Daniel Clarke Eddy

Our Travelling Party to the Alps and Rhine

Daniel Clarke Eddy

Our Travelling Party to the Alps and Rhine

ISBN/EAN: 9783743418073

Manufactured in Europe, USA, Canada, Australia, Japa

Cover: Foto ©ninafisch / pixelio.de

Manufactured and distributed by brebook publishing software (www.brebook.com)

Daniel Clarke Eddy

Our Travelling Party to the Alps and Rhine

HOSPICE OF THE GRIMSEL.

OUR TRAVELLING PARTY

TO

THE ALPS AND RHINE.

BY
DANIEL C. EDDY.

ILLUSTRATED.

BOSTON:
D. LOTHROP & COMPANY,
FRANKLIN ST., CORNER OF HAWLEY.

CONTENTS.

CHAP.		PAGE
I.	Pointed Gothic.	11
II.	Crossing the Simplon.	26
III.	The Ice-fields.	40
IV.	Taking a Bath at Leuk.	56
V.	Lake Leman.	67
VI.	Home of Calvin and Land of Tell.	84
VII.	Mammoth Organ. — Curious Clock.	98
VIII.	The Gambler's Paradise.	111
IX.	The Heights of Heidelberg.	128
X.	Frankfurt-on-the-Main.	144
XI.	On the Rhine.	156
XII.	Bishop Hatto's Tower.	169
XIII.	The Seven Sisters.	186
XIV.	Lurlei, the River Siren.	202
XV.	Rolandseck and Drachenfels.	214
XVI.	Eau de Cologne.	223
XVII.	Homeward Bound.	238

ENGRAVINGS.

	PAGE
HOSPICE OF THE GRIMSEL	1
GLACIER OF THE RHONE	10
SWISS COTTAGE	45
SWISS CHEESEMAKER	91
ZURICH	101
CONVERSATIONSHAUS	117
CASTLE OF HEIDELBERG	139
OBERWESEL	197

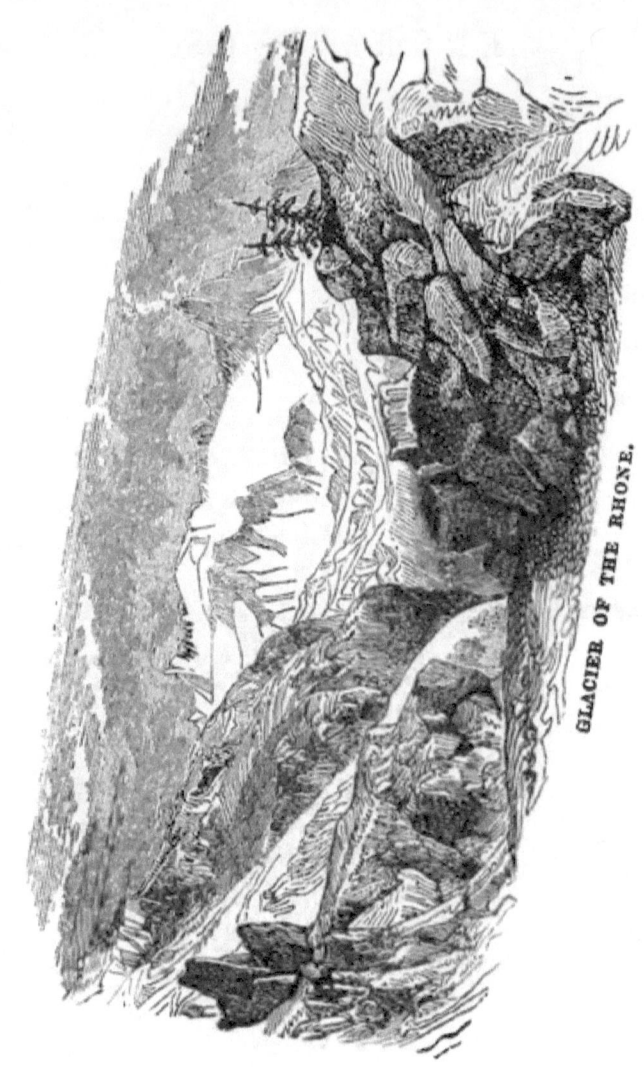

GLACIER OF THE RHONE.

THE ALPS AND THE RHINE.

Chapter I.

POINTED GOTHIC.

PERHAPS there is no journey of an equal distance in the world that has such varied scenery as a tour from the flower-decked plains of Italy, over the snow-clad Alps and seas of crystal, down the winding, arrowy Rhine, on whose banks the feudal castles stand, as grand old monuments of a buried age. Whatever may be a man's tastes, he is sure to find them gratified. If he loves the gentle slope, the green meadow, the opening vista, the dim haze, the quiet beauty of a rural scene, he will be delighted with the enchanting surroundings of Lago Maggiore and Lake Leman, or with the valleys of the Ticino or the Rhine. If he delights in the bold, rough, mountainous scenes, where sublimity seems to sit enthroned in rocky grandeur, he will find enough to satisfy him in the mountainous regions of Switzerland, where old Mont Blanc towers aloft in snowy state, the monarch of mountains. Does he love wild, awful passes, leaping cascades, and ice-hung galleries of nature? He will find them all amid the terrific scenery of the Gemmi and the Grimsel. Does he want something to lead him back to the days of chivalry, to the times of knightly valor? He will have it when he comes within sight of Rolandseck and Drachenfels.

Such a tour, embracing this grand variety, is before us in the present volume. We are at Milan, that has hardly ceased to rock with the roar of battle and the crash of arms, and the streets of which are still full of French soldiers. Before we leave it, we must go and see its central object of interest, a cathedral unlike any other in the world, and in its own style surpassing any other. St. Peter's is grander, York Minster is more impressive, but the dome of Milan is the most exquisite and tasteful of all that class of structures. At a distance it looks like a mammoth bunch of lances, and near at hand it has the appearance of a frozen city.

"This cathedral is the pride of Milan," said Mr. Percy.

"You should say, the pride of Italy," suggested Mr. Tenant.

"Beautiful!" murmured Walter to himself.

Minnie stood looking at the edifice, silent and thoughtful, and at length she exclaimed, —

"What a thing!"

"A thing?" queried Walter, looking reproachfully at her.

"Yes, bub, see those pinnacles by thousands rising in the air, one above another. It is like nothing I have ever seen."

"How beautiful the ornaments, and how elaborate the carvings!"

"See the images in the niches — one, two, three, five, ten, twenty — so many that I cannot count them."

"They are not images, sis."

"What are they, if they are not images?"

"Statues."

"Pray what is the difference, Sir Philosopher?"

"Ah, — yes, — well, — but there is a difference."

"What is it?"

"I don't hardly know, but believe the word *statue* is more commonly applied to the figure of a man in bronze and marble, while *image* is used for a figure of man or beast."

"A distinction without much difference," laughingly remarked Mr. Tenant.

"Yes," said Minnie, with some degree of sarcasm, "I understand it all, bub, a statue is an image, and an image is a statue."

Walter looked quite discomfited, while Minnie asked,—

"How many of these statues are there on the building?"

"There are seven thousand of them," replied Mr. Tenant.

"O, dear!"

"And there are niches for three or four thousand more."

"Can it be so?"

"Yes."

"How large are they?"

"Much larger than life."

"They do not look so."

"Perhaps not; but if they should be taken from the niches, you could not reach to the shoulders, even if you were as tall as I am."

"Come, let us go in," said Mr. Percy; and they all entered the cathedral.

The edifice was full of people, gathered at a funeral service of some distinguished person. The high pillars were wound around with black velvet, which only contrasted with the marble arches, and with the rich and costly decorations of the altar.

"I'm lost!" whispered Walter.

"Lost?" asked Minnie.

"Yes, I'm lost."

"Are you crazy?"

"No, I am lost in amazement."

"Then we had better send the *valet de place* to find you."

Walter laughed at Minnie's reply. The grand funeral service commenced; the solemn dirge swept through the house: the wild wail of the organ sounded like the voice of a spirit, and the impression was awful.

"When you write to mother, Walter," said Minnie afterwards, "how will you describe this cathedral?"

"I should have no language of my own that I could use."

"Whose could you borrow?"

"I know of two or three descriptions, written by travellers."

"How do they speak of it?"

"One calls it 'a forest of pinnacles with sculptured saints and angels, glittering like frostwork in the light of the setting sun —

> An aerial host
> Of figures, human and divine,
> White as the snows of Apennine
> Indurated by frost.'"

"That is good, but it does not come up to the cathedral itself."

"No language can come up to that. It seems to me to be a perfect specimen of art."

"Come, children," said Mr. Percy.

"You are not going yet — are you?" asked Walter.

"We are going up."

"Up! up! up where?" said Walter to himself.

"Up where?" shouted Minnie so loud as to be heard all around, and to call the attention of people to her.

"Why, into the dome, and on top of the building among the pinnacles," replied her father.

"All right, sir; go ahead," laughingly replied the girl, turning to Walter.

They went up over winding stairs, through dark passages and long corridors, until they were as high as they could go, and the view was grand.

"Walter, I'll tell you what I was thinking about."

"What was it, puss?"

"I was thinking that we were birds, and had made our nest up here in a forest of pinnacles, hanging or growing between earth and heaven."

"What kind of birds?"

" O, no matter what kind."

" How grand!" Walter kept saying to himself, much to the amusement of his older friends — " this sea of pinnacles, the city bathed in sunset, the distant Alps lying back against the sky, and all nature in a blaze of glory!"

While the lad was looking off upon the distant Alps, Minnie was gazing down into the city, upon the roofs and streets that seemed, from the top of the church, to be a mass of tiles and bricks. They reached the earth again just as the bells of the numerous churches were ringing for some evening festival, and entered the hotel weary with the long, hard climb up among the pinnacles of the temple.

" How will you dine — at *table d'hote*, or at a private table?" asked a servant entering the room.

" Private table," said Mr. Percy.

" I agree with you," said Mr. Tenant.

" So do I," added Walter.

" I do not, pa," said Minnie.

" Do you want to go to the *table d'hote?*"

" Yes, sir, if you will let me."

" You may, child, but you will not have so comfortable a dinner as if you should take it with us."

" Why not?"

"You know my objections to the public table. The cooking is so curious and extravagant, that to us, who are accustomed to plain food, it is not wholesome."

"I made myself sick at the common table, last time I went," said Walter.

"O, you ate too much."

"No, it was not that; I could not get enough to eat."

"Well," said Mr. Percy, "we will order our dinner, and Minnie can go down to the table."

So Walter gave Minnie his arm, and took her to the table, and gave her to the charge of an American friend there, who was accompanied by ladies, and retired. But an hour afterwards, while the three were in a private dining room, partaking of a good wholesome dinner, cooked in English style, Minnie came in.

"Ah, Min, are you here after more dinner?"

"Yes, bub."

"But you have been to the table there an hour."

"I know it."

"And have not had enough?"

"No; let me sit down at your table."

"You may, sis," said Mr. Tenant, "if you will confess the leanness of the *table d'hote*, and give a description of what you dined on."

"Well, I will."

"Begin then."

"No; fill my plate first."

The plate was filled, and Minnie gave a description.

"I will give the courses in order, as near as I can remember. First dish was rice soup, about two table spoonfuls, and the moment the plate was empty it was hurried away; roast beef, a piece two inches square, very thin and very lean, dry and highly spiced; a little pie about as large as a silver dollar, — it might have been rat pie, for all I could tell; a small bird, hardly larger than a canary, all bones, stuffed with burning spices; a little piece of mutton, very nice, very small, and very soon eaten; salad with fixings, in homœopathic doses; jelly in such limited quantity that whoever took all he wanted would take the whole."

"Bah, do stop," cried Walter.

The little girl did stop, and ate a very nice dinner with her friends, and declared she never would go to the public table again, if she could help it.

Here at Milan is an old amphitheatre, in a good state of preservation. It will accommodate thirty-two thousand persons, and has a spacious arena, which was once used for gladiatorial exhibitions. When our party was there it was all decorated with red and gold for a public festival. The arena had been flooded, and there was to be a naval engagement for the amusement of the people. As the children saw the extensive preparations that were being made, they were enthusiastic.

"We will all go," said Minnie.

"Yes," replied her brother, "we would not lose this spectacle for any thing."

"There is one unfortunate thing about it," said Mr. Percy.

"What is that?" asked both children at once.

"The exhibition comes on Sunday."

"Sunday?"

"Yes."

"What! on the Lord's day?" asked Walter in astonishment.

"I should think," said his father, "that you had travelled enough to know that in Europe not much reverence and respect are paid to the Sabbath."

"I know that, but did not suppose a public structure like this would be open on the Sabbath, especially as it is just beneath the shadow of that awe-inspiring cathedral."

"Do you want to go to-morrow afternoon?"

"No, pa, you know we do not. If we should go to such an entertainment on Sunday, knowing, as we do in relation to this one, what we should see, we should not dare to meet our dear mother again, and look into her face," said Minnie earnestly.

"I am glad you think of your mother. Her kind heart would be pained if she knew you violated the Sabbath. The separation of months is enough without her hearing that you have used the Sabbath for an unholy purpose."

"Then," added Walter, "I remember what God has said."

"What?" asked Minnie.

"'Remember the Sabbath day, to keep it holy.'"

"I will take you this afternoon to an exhibition which will interest you."

"What is it?" asked they both.

"You remember the picture in the west room of our house in Cambridge, over the mantel."

"Yes, sir."

"What is it?"

"A steel plate engraving of the 'Last Supper.'"

"Do you know who originated the picture?"

"No, sir," answered Minnie.

"Do you, my son?"

"Yes, sir; it is engraved from a painting of Leonardo da Vinci."

"Can you tell me who he was?"

"Only that he was a noted painter."

"Can you tell us any thing about him, father?" asked Minnie.

"Yes, he was born in 1451, and ——"

"What does *da* stand for in his name?"

"Wait and I will tell you. He was a native of Vinci. *Da* means *of*. He was Leonardo of the town of Vinci."

"Ah, ha! that is it, then."

"Though he was a painter of great eminence, he did not devote his time wholly to that art."

"What did he do?"

"He was in public life, and held some offices under the government, and the painting of the Last Supper is nearly all that remains of his works."

"Is that painting in Milan?"

"Yes."

"Where?"

"It is on the wall of an old convent of the Dominicans of Sta. Maria delle Grazie."

"Shall we see it?"

"Yes; the convent is now used for barracks, but we will go there."

After dinner they rode out, and found the

monastery, and went into the refectory where the fresco is. It has been retouched and amended until its former beauty is injured if not destroyed. Many persons were there to look at it, and the gentlemen of our party studied it for a long time.

"I remember," said Mr. Tenant, "what Prime says about the central figure in this group, — the Saviour."

"What does he say?" asked Mr. Percy.

"He says, in an enthusiastic description of this picture, that 'the head of the Christ is the only head that ever came up to his conception of the Saviour's. Rubens and Raphael never satisfied him, but when he saw in this face the God and the man so blended, he cried out, My Lord, and my God!'"

"That is high praise, but deserved."

"Yes, I think so."

Walter bought an engraving of the painting by Raphael Morghen, and they left the monastery, and rode towards the centre of the city. As they rode along, Mr. Tenant put to Minnie the following question: —

"Do you know why an establishment where bonnets are made and sold is called a *millinery* establishment?"

"No, sir."

"You young ladies, who deal so much in millinery articles, should know."

"Should?"

"Certainly."

"Then, perhaps, you can tell me why that ugly-looking steeple top you have on your head is called *hat*."

"The word from which it is derived signifies *to defend* or *ward off*."

"Walter and I," said the little girl, "vote that answer unsatisfactory, because your steeple top is always in the way, an incumbrance rather than a shield. But about millinery."

"The word comes from this place. Long ago this kind of work was done here to a great extent, and thus the name *Milan*-ery was given to that branch of industry."

"That is a fact worth remembering."

"What will you remember most in this place?" asked Walter of his sister.

"I don't know, and I am sure I couldn't tell. What shall you remember most distinctly?"

"The cathedral."

"O, yes."

"It is so unique, and unlike any thing else that we have seen, that it is engraved on my memory; and should I live a hundred years, I should never lose from my recollection the outlines and grand filling up of this noble structure, which I have described in a letter to mother, under the head of "POINTED GOTHIC."

The children were very sure that they should never forget this cathedral, and seldom does any one who ever looks on it forget its glorious outlines and its elaborate finish. Once seen it is never to be forgotten. It fixes itself in the mind, stamps itself in the memory, and years after the visit to Milan is made the traveller calls up, as one of the notable days of his life, that on which he stood and gazed upon that grand consummation of architectural beauty.

Chapter II.

CROSSING THE SIMPLON.

"CROSSING the Simplon! I thought you were going over the Alps," said Minnie, as the party left the hotel in Milan to take the cars for the Simplon.

"Min, you are a simple-ton!" replied Walter.

"Quite complimentary, bub! But why am I a simpleton?"

"Because, after all we have talked about it, you do not understand where we are going."

"We are going over the Simplon; I understand that."

"And the Simplon is a pass over the Alps, Simplon being the name of one single mountain, and Alps the name of the whole ridge."

"Ah, ha!"

"Here we are at the diligence office,— an early start,— five o'clock in the morning," said Mr. Tenant.

They took seats in the omnibus, and were soon on their way. The road was admirable, and the horses tolerable, and the progress about five miles an hour. When they arrived at Novara they found a train of cars just starting for Arona, and took seats at once. When they reached Arona, which is on Lago Maggiore, they met with some trouble, and were furnished with some amusement, mingled with vexation. On leaving the cars they found a steamer just ready to sail, but they did not know where she went. They expected to find a diligence, but it did not appear, and they could find no one who could converse in French or English. They did not dare to take the steamer, and they could not find the stage. They went to a hotel, but failed to make any body understand what they wanted, and for a while stood in the street undecided which way to go. The steamer left her anchorage and went puffing over the lake, and the prospect of our travellers getting on was any thing but favorable. They asked a well-dressed man who was passing by, but he only laughed at them: the boys in the street gathered around the party and hooted: ragged men with their hands in their pockets, and dirty women with pipes in their mouths, came out of the houses and stood around them with shrugs and expressive gestures. Mr. Tenant came nearer losing his temper than at any time during the journey.

"Miserable town!" he exclaimed.

"Miserable people, I should think," replied Mr. Percy.

"Ah, pa," said Minnie, "the people look very good-natured and hospitable. We seem to be the miserable ones."

They all laughed at this, and the frown faded from Mr. Tenant's face. He was provoked with the people, and thought them very stupid, when the trouble was with himself in being enraged at meeting annoyances in travelling through a country the language of which he did not understand. But soon a diligence came in sight, and Mr. Percy turned to ask where it was going to, but did not succeed in finding out.

"Is that diligence going to the Simplon?"

The people shook their heads.

"To Milan?"

They shook their heads

"To Novara?"

They shook their heads.

"Stupid dolts!"

They shook their heads.

The diligence had now reached the place where they stood, and the driver, seeing a crowd in the street, stopped to ascertain what it was. Our party appealed to him, but could not make him understand any thing.

He yelled in Italian.

They conversed in English and French.

At last Mr. Tenant caught up his carpet bag and threw it upon the diligence, and ordered the driver to put on the rest of the baggage.

"I am going in this shabby vehicle," he said.

"Where?" asked Mr. Percy.

"Any where."

"But it may not be going where we want to go to."

"I don't care much where it goes to, as long as it goes out of this miserable, dirty town."

"Well, we will go with you."

They all got into the diligence, and found just seats enough for themselves. They did not know where they were going, and for a time did not dare to ask.

"Mr. Tenant," said Minnie, "you are decidedly out of sorts."

"Who could help being out of sorts — mad, if you will have it so?"

"I could."

"Ah!"

"Yes, sir."

Mr. Percy soon thought it time to inquire where the diligence was going to. He found a man who could converse in French, and from him learned that the party were in the right carriage and on their way in the right direction.

This restored the good feelings of all; and the cloud swept away even from Mr. Tenant's brow, who had been more distracted than usual. He was generally the coolest and most dispassionate of the whole company. From two o'clock until eight in the evening they rode on, through a country of surpassing loveliness. The lower Alps were soon seen, and in the hazy atmosphere presented an ever-varying appearance, now rough and rugged, and then the smoothly-rounded cone; now bare and desolate, and anon crowned with verdure and covered with foliage. The road all along was delightful and pleasant. Formed for the march of armies, it was broad, smooth, level, and destitute of ruts and gullies. It winds around the base of the mountains, whose sides are covered with vines and foliage of various kinds, from out of which peep, now and then, the cottage of the peasant, the church-tower, and the humble, unostentatious village, and whose summits are concealed by the ever shifting clouds. The children were very much pleased, especially as they rode along the shores of Lake Maggiore, within sight of the picturesque Island of Isola Bella, the seat of Count Borromeo, which rises from the bosom of the dark wave like a star shining through a night cloud.

At eight o'clock they reached Domo d'Ossola, a mean Italian town just at the foot of the Simplon.

"What a place!" exclaimed Mr. Percy.

"A place, indeed!" replied Mr. Tenant; "one traveller describes it as 'a dirty town, with a smell of garlic, and red-capped, mahogany-legged, lazy lazzaroni lounging through the streets.'"

"I smell the garlic, Mr. Tenant," said Minnie.

"And I have seen the red-capped lazzaroni," added Walter.

"Supper ready!" from Mr. Percy, interrupted their uncomplimentary remarks, and they went into the little dining room of the hotel, in front of which they had been conversing, where they had beefsteak and coffee, of the character of which an opinion may be formed by the following remarks: —

"This steak tastes as if it had been cooked on ashes," said Mr. Tenant.

"The coffee looks as if it was made of ink," added Mr. Percy.

"The eggs taste as if they were laid by the hens that Noah carried into the ark."

The gentlemen laughed at Minnie's comment on the eggs, but Walter replied, —

"I find the steak palatable, the coffee tolerable, and the eggs decidedly good."

"I guess you are hungry, Walter," said Minnie.

"Yes."

"And you eat with your eyes shut."

"Yes."

"Then, perhaps, you can relish your supper."

The party were now called to the diligence, which was about to start. They arrived at the foot of the Simplon, and entered the grand pass, just at nightfall, and, until nine the next morning, continued to ascend over the splendid road which the genius of Napoleon built amid those frowning heights, and over which his armies passed in midwinter, now overwhelmed by the avalanche, and anon emerging from the danger, to pour themselves upon the smiling fields below. The scenery was wild and awful. On one side towered the high peaks, from which swept down the cold, icy wind; on the other side were deep ravines and terrible precipices, which yawned as if eager to devour an army. Now they passed the refuge houses; the convent, at the gate of which stood a large St. Bernard dog, ready for duty; beautiful cascades leaping down from cliff to cliff; piles of snow in midsummer; and many a huge rock projecting overhead, and ready to fall upon the head of the traveller.

Yet up, up, they went, until they reached the

Gorge of Gondo, a magnificent gallery, cut five hundred and ninety-six feet through the hard rock, down over which the water tumbles with ceaseless roar. For a while they stood in that gorge wondering and amazed at what they saw, and then went on again to new scenes. All that night they continued to climb, the impressions of awe becoming deeper every moment. There is every thing in that wild scene to make one forget the narrow occupations of earth, and lift up his soul to God. The stupendous heights; the yawning caverns; the everlasting roar of the descending torrents; the dark night and the dawning morning; the hospice of the monks; the exposure to the descending avalanche; the galleries hewn out of solid rock, dripping with water and hung with icicles; the wet, misty clouds which now sweep down upon us, and anon roll back, and leave the traveller in moonlight and starlight, — all increase the interest and awfulness of the ascent. The cold was intense, though not greater than they expected. The snow was lying in drifts on the sides of the mountains, and above them, in the gorges, shone the glaciers.

At day dawn they reached the tavern on the Simplon, where they took breakfast. The fare was poor, but the ride of the night had made the appetite excellent, and the coarse bread and honey set before the hungry tourists were devoured speedily. From this point the two gentlemen, with Walter, walked to the highest grade of the pass, and at length the cross, which marks the turning-point, standing in its loneliness, was seen — a truthful emblem, suggesting holy thoughts to the travellers in their dreary march. As Walter ran ahead with another young man, who, with our party, left the diligence behind, Mr. Tenant, making a snow ball, threw it at the lad, and nearly took off his cap.

"Ah," said Walter, turning round, "that is your game — is it?"

Just as he said so a huge mass of snow, thrown by Mr. Tenant, came full in his face, almost smothering him. He uttered a quick cry, above which arose the merry shout of the perpetrator of the act. But Walter rallied, and brushed the snow from his face.

"It is a poor rule that won't work both ways," he said, as he caught up some snow and formed it into snowballs, and threw them with great rapidity at Mr. Tenant. The young man with Walter also went into the fun with much zeal, and soon it became a drawn game between Walter and his young friend on one side, and the two gentlemen on the other. For about five minutes a vigorous snowballing was kept up in grand style. At length a well-directed ball from the hand of Walter struck the hat of Mr. Tenant, and taking it from his head, sent it over the cliff into the valley below.

"Gone," said Mr. Tenant.

"That is so," added Mr. Percy.

"Can't I get it?" asked Walter, sobered down at once from his hilarity by the event.

"No, it is gone."

"I am sorry, indeed I am."

"It is not your fault, Walter," said Mr. Tenant; "I commenced the game. I wanted to have some snowballing on the Alps in midsummer, and have had it."

"Yes, but I knocked off your hat."

"I know it, and though I regret the loss of that, yet even at that expense I would not lose the exhilaration of the game of snowballing."

Mr. Tenant tied a silk handkerchief around his head, and waited for the diligence to come up. Among his baggage he had a cap, which he put on, and was well laughed at by Minnie for his defeat, as she called it, in his game with Walter.

"How high are we?" asked Walter of his father, when the excitement of the snowballing had subsided.

"The Simplon pass is about six thousand seven hundred feet."

"What is the St. Gothard."

"Six thousand eight hundred feet."

"What is the Splugen?"

"The same as the St. Gothard."

"What is the Great Bernard?"

"About eight thousand feet."

"I have read," said Minnie, "so much about the Alpine passes, that I thought it more dangerous to cross than we have found it."

"There is little danger in summer."

"But what made M'Donald's pass so terrible?"

"He crossed long before these roads were laid out, making a road for himself. He crossed, too, in midwinter."

"Well, I never had any correct idea of what it was to cross the Alps. I wish you would explain to me something about the avalanches that I have heard of."

"One who has never seen this region of ice," said Mr. Percy, "can hardly have a conception of it. Here, in the heat of summer, while the fertile plains of Italy, and the vineyards of France, and the orchards of Germany are blushing with flowers, hanging with fruit, and radiant with beauty, these everlasting piles of sunless snow and ice remain in mountainous forms, unmelted from age to age, and commanding the wonder of all who gaze upon them. The avalanches are of two kinds. One is called the dust avalanche, which consists of masses of loose, light snow, which gets shaken together by the wind, and then begins to roll down the mountain, turning and increasing in size as it comes, until to the people who see it from below it seems as if the mountain itself was turning over and rolling down towards you. But the danger of these is comparatively small. They generally break, and lose their power before they have accomplished much mischief. But there is another kind. These are composed of masses of hard ice, that become detached from the main masses by the action of the water. Sometimes the ice lays in layers, and the top layer of acres is at once dislodged, and comes thundering down the mountain sides. Then woe to whatever stands in the way of this terrible agent of ruin. On, on, it comes; villages are in its path, but they are swept away as if they were made of glass; trees are torn up by the wind that the formidable mass sets in motion; fearful explosions take place as the ice cracks and breaks, and the devastation is perfect. The traveller over the Alps is sometimes startled with what appears to him like distant thunder in one continuous roll. He turns his eye upon the neighboring mountain, and sees one of these avalanches pouring itself down upon the plains below, assuming all kinds of fantastic shapes, dashing on as if the earth itself was to be overwhelmed. He thanks God, even if he be a sceptic, that he is not in the path of that awful power, which armies could not avert, which no walls of iron or stone could turn aside."

They were now descending the mountains on the Swiss side, rattling along, now holding on to the side of the rickety diligence, anon bursting forth with exclamations of surprise at the grand and awful scenes around them. On their way they came to Brieg, a town that occupies the position at the foot of the mountain on one side that Domo d'Ossola does on the other side. They tarried here only long enough to dine, and then pressed on to Martigny.

The baggage was thrown from the diligence with violence at the door of one of the hotels, but when Mr. Tenant entered and asked for apartments, they were not to be had. The house was all full, and the answers to the numerous questions asked were not very courteous. They tried one or two public houses and received the answer,

"All full."

"We will sleep on lounges or on the floor."

"All full."

At length they found a hotel that was not full, and it proved to be the best in the mean little town, and there found a home for the night.

It was very hard for the children to sleep. They had seen so much, and anticipated so much, that they were restless and wakeful, though they had no rest the night previous. Walter, as soon as he fell asleep, began to dream of falling from a high precipice, and cried out so loud that his father was obliged to wake him. Soon he was asleep again, dreaming about avalanches and snow storms. So all night in his dreams he was among frightful dangers, and tottering over steep mountains. Minnie did not sleep much better, but groaned in her dreams so hard that her father began to fear that she was sick.

Chapter III.

THE ICE FIELDS.

EARLY the next morning all was interest and excitement. The two children were up before the sun, and when breakfast was ready had talked over their plans for the day with the most intense satisfaction. When the morning meal was finished, the whole company, prepared to visit the fields of ice, stood in front of the hotel. Minnie was put upon a mule, and a guide stood at the bridle. Walter was similarly mounted, and a guide walked by his side. The two gentlemen told their guides to go behind. Thus the party started, while a great crowd stood looking on with as much interest as if a like scene had not been witnessed a thousand times. As they moved slowly on, at mule pace, they had time for conversation, and many were the questions asked by the children about the ice fields.

"What are those long poles which the guides carry called, father," asked Minnie.

"They are Alpine-stocks."

"What are glaciers?"

"They are immense fields of ice, and the ice differs from common ice, being little particles of congealed snow."

"Are glaciers very extensive among the Alps?"

"Yes, there are said to be, in Switzerland and its immediate neighborhood, about one thousand five hundred square miles of glacier surface."

"What is the most famous?"

"The *Mer de Glace*."

"What does *Mer de Glace* mean?"

"Sea of glass."

"O! How extensive is that?"

"It is many miles long."

"Shall I see the glaciers?"

"You will see enough to satisfy you."

"Please tell me more about them."

"What do you want to know?"

"Why, how they are formed, how they look, and what they are like. I have heard so much about them that I want to learn all I can."

"Well, drive your mule up as near me as possible, and I will tell you."

"There, I can hear every word you say."

"The glaciers are formed by the melting of the snow, and the water, freezing, forms vast flakes or fields of crystal. Glaciers are found at about eight thousand feet elevation: above are the snow regions, pure, white, unsullied. The action of cold and heat throws these glaciers into different shapes and forms. Sometimes they rise like a castle with its towers and turrets; sometimes they are spread out like vast fields of colored glass, beautiful to the eye, and inspiring the imagination with a thousand fancies. When these glaciers begin to move, they come down into the valleys, fill them up, and so change the atmosphere that summer is not long enough to melt them out, and there they lie from age to age. The famous *Mer de Glace* was thus formed, and the mountain gorge, visited now by so many travellers as a field of ice, was once a blooming Swiss valley."

" Can it be ? "

" So it is supposed."

They now began to ascend the Forclaz. Mr. Tenant was leading the way, and Walter followed, singing at the top of his voice, to a very unmusical tune, —

" Mont Blanc is the monarch of mountains;
  They crowned him long ago
On a throne of rocks in a robe of clouds,
  With a diadem of snow.
Around his waist are forests braced,
  The avalanche in his hand;

> But ere it fall, that thundering ball
>   Must pause for my command.
> The glacier's cold and restless mass
>   Moves onward day by day;
> But I am he who bids it pass,
>   Or makes its ice delay.
> I am the spirit of the place,
>   Could make the mountain bow
> And quiver to his caverned base —
>   And what with me wouldst *thou?*"

The way was very rough, and to these travellers seemed very dangerous; and fifty times Minnie wished she had not come, though she was not willing to confess it. Her mule did not stumble, though he bore her along the edge of tremendous precipices, and her little heart trembled as she saw the peril to which she was exposed. If Walter felt any fear he did not manifest it by word or look. He was calmly engaged in contemplating the grandeur of the scene. The pass was made, and the party descended safely into the *Val du Trient*, and stopped at a neat Swiss cottage, and took some refreshments. Minnie, being very weary, went to bed, and the rest of the company resolved upon an excursion suggested by the guides. They were soon upon the Forclaz, some four thousand feet above the level of the sea, in the midst of scenes of indescribable grandeur. In one direction they could look off upon the town of Martigny, which they left that morning. At length they returned, and taking Minnie with them, went on. All at once Walter, who was in advance of the rest, shouted,—

" Eureka ! Eureka ! "

" What have you found now ? " asked Mr. Tenant, riding up.

" The most beautiful prospect in the world."

" Pho."

" Come and see it."

" Grand ! " was the exclamation of the gentleman, as he reached Walter's side, and saw what had called forth the lad's enthusiasm.

There, far down below, was the valley of Chamouni, while seeming to rise above it, as if about to descend upon it, was old Mont Blanc, the monarch mountain, all misty and dim, and having on the everlasting nightcap of snow and ice.

" Now the rest of the way will be easy," said Minnie, who had had about enough of glaciers.

" What makes you think so ? " asked her father.

" Because it is all down hill."

" That may be a reason why it will be more difficult."

" O, mercy ! " cried the child.

SWISS COTTAGE.

"What? what?"

They all turned to where Minnie pointed with her finger, and were in consternation to see that the mule on which Mr. Tenant rode had lost his footing, and that both beast and rider were rolling over in the soft snow. For a moment a terrible fear stopped their very breath as they gazed upon the scene.

"He is safe," cried Mr. Percy, relieving the fears of the children at once, as he saw Mr. Tenant regain his feet. The mule also saved himself, and when the others reached the place where Mr. Tenant was, that gentleman was mounted and ready to rejoin them, having learned a lesson of experience, and narrowly escaped with his life.

"Did you hurt you?" asked Minnie.

"Not much."

"How came you to fall?"

"It was my carelessness; I drove the mule faster than it was safe for him to go."

They reached Chamouni that night, having had a wild but interesting and toilsome day. Minnie better understood what glaciers are than she did in the morning, and Walter had his head full of information and interesting particulars. At Chamouni, Minnie was turned over to the care of several American ladies who were there, and the other three persons of the party spent a week in climbing about among these mountains of snow and ice. When they went to *Mer de Glace,* Walter had a pair of strong shoes, with iron nails in them, on his feet, and he had a pair of green spectacles on his face. The object of the spectacles was to save his eyes from the glare of the ice, which often seriously affects the sight. At night, when they returned, the boy told his sister that in all his travels he had never seen any thing like *Mer de Glace.*

" Was it grander than the ocean ? " she asked.

" Yes, it was."

" Was it grander than the mountains of Southern Austria, over which we rode ? "

" Yes."

" Grander than St. Peter's."

" Pho! St. Peter's! a playhouse! what is that to what I have seen to-day ? "

" Grander than Vesuvius ? "

" Yes — about — quite — a little more — I don't know."

" Well, that is an intelligible answer, truly."

" I think it *is* grander than Vesuvius."

" Well, that is a straightforward answer."

During the time spent at Chamouni, the gentlemen of the party saw much of the wild scenery of the Alps. They tried the pass of the

Tête Noire, slept a night in the hospice of the Grimsel, went up the Jungfrau, became acquainted with the monks of St. Bernard, met with several hair-breadth escapes and remarkable adventures. At length they found themselves all united again at Martigny, where the guides were paid and discharged, and preparations were made to go on into Switzerland. The night after the arrival of the company at Martigny, Walter awoke with a terrible feeling in his feet. He tried to sleep, but could not. The pain became more and more intolerable, until he could endure it no longer.

"Father," he called to Mr. Percy, who slept in an adjoining room. "Father!"

"Hey? what? who calls?" inquired Mr. Percy, half awake.

"Father, I call."

"You, my son?"

"Yes, sir."

"What is the matter?"

"I don't know."

"Then go to sleep."

"I cannot sleep."

"Why not?"

"My feet feel very bad. They are in great pain."

"What is the matter with them?"

"I cannot tell you."

"Well, they are tired. Go to sleep, and they will be well in the morning."

He tried to sleep, but the more he tried the more he could not, and at length called again, —

"Father."

"What say?"

"Please come and see what the matter is with my feet."

"Don't they feel any better?"

"No, sir."

Mr. Percy came into Walter's room, got a candle, and looked at the poor boy's feet.

"Something is the matter," he said.

"How do they look?"

"Badly, my son."

"They feel very badly."

"They must be attended to."

He rang the bell, and the sound was heard through the silent house.

"Tinkle, tinkle, tinkle."

Nobody answered.

"Tinkle, tinkle, tinkle," again.

No response.

"Tinkle, tinkle, tinkle," still louder.

Soon a tread was heard in the hall, and a knock at the door.

" Come in."

" What is wanted, sir ? "

" Have you a physician in the house ? "

" No."

" Can you tell what is the trouble with this poor lad's feet ? "

" Let me see them."

The servant looked at Walter's feet, and his countenance lighted as he said, —

" I know."

" What is it ? "

" They are only snow-blistered."

" *Only!* " groaned Walter.

" What can you do for them ? " asked Mr. Percy.

" Cure them."

" That is good — do it."

The servant ran out and obtained a preparation of brandy and some other articles, and at once proceeded to bathe the feet of the suffering boy, who soon, under the operation, fell asleep, and woke in the morning with his feet nearly as well as ever.

Then they were ready to leave Martigny, and taking the diligence, — *dilatory* as Minnie persisted in calling it, — started for Geneva.

" This is a wonderful country," said Mr. Tenant, as they were riding along.

"Yes," answered Mr. Percy. "Rousseau says that in Switzerland 'nature unites all seasons in one instant, all climates in one spot.'"

"Very true."

"Father," said Minnie.

"What is it, child?"

"I want to know one thing."

"Two things you shall know if I can tell you."

"Only one at a time."

"What is that?"

"What is the dreadful swelling I see on the necks of the people here?"

"It is called the 'goitre.'"

"What is the cause of it?"

"The cause is not known fully."

"What is *supposed* to be the cause?"

"Some attribute it to the use of snow water."

"Is it never found when snow water is not drank."

"Yes."

"Then it cannot be that."

"There are also many cretins found here."

"What are 'cretins'?"

"Idiots."

"Are they numerous."

"Yes, Walter met seventeen in passing through one village."

"What produces cretins?"

"That is as much unknown as the cause of the goitre."

"How terrible!"

"I have seen these goitres in America and in England."

"What part of England do you find them in?"

"They are found in Yorkshire, Derbyshire, and in other parts of England, in limestone districts mostly."

"Is it called goitre in England and America?"

"I have never heard any name given to it in our country, but in England it is called the 'Derbyshire neck.'"

"Does the same cause produce the goitre and idiocy both?"

"Probably."

"What do scientific men say about it?"

"I remember what Coxe says."

"What?"

"He says, 'The same causes which generate goitres *probably* operate in the case of idiots; for wherever goitres prevail to a considerable degree, idiots invariably abound; such is the nice and inexplicable connection between our bodies and our minds, that the one ever sympathizes with the other; and it is by no means an ill-grounded conjecture, that the same causes which affect the body should also affect the mind; or, in other words, that the waters which created obstructions and goitres should also occasion mental imbecility. Although these idiots are frequently the children of goitrous parents, and have usually those swellings themselves, yet they are sometimes the offspring even of healthy parents, whose other children are properly organized, and are themselves free from guttural excrescences. I observed several children, scarcely ten years old, with very large goitres. These tumors, when they increase to a considerable magnitude, check perspiration, and render those who are afflicted with them exceedingly indolent and languid.'"

"O, dear me! I should not want to live here."

"Ah, you change your tune," said Walter; "yesterday you were wishing you could live in this country all your days."

"But how should I look with a goitre on my neck?"

"It would not improve your beauty — your looks, I mean. As to beauty, you cannot boast of——"

"There, take that, bub, for your impudence;" cried the child, snapping her brother on the ear.

"Just as I mean, Min."

"Well, Master Walter, if you wish to banter,

let me ask how you would appear if you were a cretin."

"I don't know."

"Never mind, children," said Mr. Percy; "thank the wise and good Father that you have neither of these dreadful maladies; that the goitre does not abound where you live, and that idiocy has not afflicted either of you."

Then Mr. Percy endeavored to impress on the minds of his young charge the obligations to gratitude under which they were placed, in consequence of having been endowed with reason, intelligence, health, and having received their existence in a land where there are so many blessings lavished alike on rich and poor. Amid those sublime exhibitions of nature it was easy for Mr. Percy to turn the thoughts of his children up to God, and from the wonderful creation itself they were directed to the infinite, unseen Creator, who is the same yesterday, to-day, and forever, whose existence has no past, no future, but is ever present; whose name is I Am.

Chapter IV.

Taking a Bath at Leuk.

"Leuk?" queried Walter to himself, as he heard his father say they should stop at Leuk. "What is there, I wonder?"

"Father," he added, "why do you stop at Leuk?"

"To take a bath, my son."

"A bath?"

"Yes."

"I should not think you would stop for that. We have had bathing enough all through these mountainous regions."

"It is not merely for *a* bath that we stop."

"What is it then?"

"There are some singular things about the bath that we wish to stop for."

"Then the baths of Leuk have medicinal qualities."

"Yes, they are said to have."

"I shall be glad to stop if there is any thing to see."

"You will find enough to amuse you at

Leuk, for such bathing you have never seen before."

Leuk is a small village, which the traveller passes on his way from the Simplon to Geneva. The hot springs are about four thousand six hundred feet above the sea, and the way to them is difficult. But they are said to have many virtues, and invalids resort to them in great numbers. Our travellers were induced to visit them only from motives of curiosity. The way to the springs is cut in the rock, and one takes a sweat in getting to them.

"A man must have the rheumatism very obstinately," said Mr. Tenant, "if it does not yield to the exertion of getting up to these baths."

"Your collar is yielding, Mr. Tenant," said Minnie.

"Is it?" asked he, feeling for his collar, which was all wilted down.

After some exertion they reached the baths, and entering an anteroom, the regulations, in French, were put into their hands.

"Read them, Walter — can you?" asked his father.

"I will try, sir."

Walter read on a while, as well as he could, translating as he read.

"Ah, Mr. Tenant, here is one rule that will apply to you."

"What is it about?"

"It relates to corpulent persons."

"But I am not corpulent."

"No; but it also relates to heavy persons. You are tall and of good weight."

"Read it, and let me judge."

"Here it is: 'For a person over ten years of age four porters are necessary; if he is above the ordinary weight, six porters; but if he is of an *extraordinary* weight, and the commissary judges proper, two others may be added, but never more.'"

"That must apply to persons more corpulent and weighty than any of us."

"But what does that mean?" asked Minnie.

"You will understand when you get through this establishment. You know that heavy persons are carried up the steep steps cut in the stones. They are assisted in their bathing arrangements, I suppose; but we shall see."

"Walter, is there no regulation that applies to me?" asked Minnie.

"Yes."

"Read it."

"This will apply to you: 'A fine of two francs will be imposed on any one who does not conduct in a proper manner while in this building, or is guilty of any impropriety in entering or leaving the bath.'"

"Now, that is impudent!"

"What is impudent?" asked Walter.

"Why, that rule."

"What is there wrong about the rule?"

"Not the rule. I didn't mean that, but the application of the rule to me."

"That is where the shoe pinches, Min."

"Yes."

"Well, here is another rule: 'No one is permitted to enter these baths without being clothed in a long, ample, and thick mantle, under the penalty of a fine of two francs.'"

Having examined the rules, the two gentlemen decided not to bathe, but the children thought they would try it. As they were not under the physician's care, they were not limited as to the length of time they were to remain in the water. Suitably arrayed, the children entered the bath together. It had a temperature of one hundred and twenty degrees of Fahrenheit; and was any thing but comfortable. Benches are under the water, so that bathers can sit down; and as those who are sick often remain in six or eight hours, they are obliged to take their meals in the water. The two gentlemen went in and sat down in a little gallery around the bath, where they could converse with the children, who soon pleaded to be taken out. They had had enough of the Leuk baths.

"I don't see why people should like to come here," said Minnie, as she stood with the rest of the party, an hour afterwards, looking at the bathers.

"Nor I," added Walter.

"I suppose," said their father, "that they do not come here for pleasure, but for health."

"Have you ever heard of any one who has been cured here?"

"No; but the waters are medicinal, and Dr. John Forbes says, 'The baths are employed for many chronic diseases, but their greatest reputation is in cutaneous diseases, scrofula, chronic rheumatism, and indolent gout. Of their great efficacy in many such cases, as well as in others of a different description, we have sufficient proof in actual experience; and this is a result that might be fairly expected from so powerful an agency as hot water, when applied in the manner it is applied here. Immersion in a fluid of a temperature approaching or exceeding that of the human blood, for a fourth or third part of every twenty-four hours, during the space of a month or two, *must* produce some important modification in the actual condition of the animal functions; and it would be strange if this modification were not sometimes beneficial, as well as sometimes injurious. It could be easily shown, on physiological grounds, how this should be so, as it is known by actual experiment to be so.'"

"I wish I knew all the arrangements here."

"I have a paper in my hand which gives them to some extent."

"Read it, pa," said Minnie.

"Walter may."

Walter took the paper, and read in a voice distinct enough to be heard by the company, and yet too low to disturb others, the following statement of the manner of conducting the baths, to every word of which Minnie listened: 'The full routine of bathing occupies no less than eight hours a day. The patients enter at four o'clock in the morning; at six o'clock coffee is placed on the floating tables, for those who like it, and at eight o'clock they retire, partake generally of a good breakfast, and then return to bed for two hours. At twelve o'clock they reenter the bath, remain there for four hours, and to this succeeds another hour's bed, dinner *ad libitum*, and an hour's good walking on the promenade. In the evening balls and concerts relieve the ennui of fashionable life. There are lodging houses and baths, supported by voluntary contributions, for the poor Germans. The treatment is reputed to be oppressive to the spirits, and very debilitating. One might suppose that it would be resorted to only when all other expedients had failed; but this, assuredly, is not the case. During the season, which lasts for three or four months, the hotels are generally pretty well filled with French and Swiss visitors, and a few Germans. For the rest of the year all the doors and windows of the hotels are boarded up, and the place is almost deserted, from its being at such an elevation on the mountains.'"

"Ugh!" exclaimed Minnie.

"What is the matter?" asked Walter.

"Why, to think I have been in that bath!"

"What of it?"

"With people who have all kinds of diseases. No knowing but I have caught something."

The gentlemen laughed at her, and in the laugh she joined; and soon they all left the baths, and were on board the diligence towards Geneva. Having rode to Bex they dined, and took the cars for Villeneuve. A circumstance took place at Bex which was pleasing to them all. As Mr. Tenant was purchasing the car tickets, just before starting, he had a little conversation with the ticket master; at the close of which a gentleman, accompanied by a tall, pale lady, dressed in deep mourning, approached him and said, —

"Allow me to ask, sir, are you an Englishman?"

"No, sir, an American," replied Mr. Tenant.

"Ah, I am happy to meet with you. I am an American myself. What part of the States are you from?"

"From Cambridge, Massachusetts."

"I am from the Granite State."

"Ah, I was born there. God bless the noble state! Here is my card," handing the stranger a card with his (Mr. Tenant's) name on it.

"I am Franklin Pierce," said the stranger, who at once entered into conversation with Mr. Tenant.

"Minnie, Minnie!" said Walter, who had listened to the above conversation.

"What, bub?"

"That gentleman talking with Mr. Tenant — and now being introduced to father — is Ex-President Pierce."

"You don't say so, though."

"He said his name was Franklin Pierce."

"That may be. If he had said his name was George Washington, that would not have proved him to be the first president of our country."

"No; but this gentleman looks like pictures which I have seen of the ex-president."

"I have never seen any."

"I must find out;" and the boy drew nearer the gentlemen, and Mr. Percy, seeing him, said, "Come here, children;" and then turning to the stranger, he added, "These are my children, who are travelling with us, President Pierce."

The ex-president at once took the hands of the children, asking them how they liked to travel so far away from home, what they had seen in their tour, and when they were to return home. All these questions the children answered in such an intelligent manner that the distinguished gentleman seemed much pleased.

As the cars were about to start, Mr. Pierce said, "We should be pleased to take seats in the same car with you;" and with this arrangement the whole Percy party was much pleased.

When seated in the cars the conversation turned on home and native land; and the children listened with much pleasure to the enthusiastic declarations of the distinguished personage once at the head of the government, that of the United States, is the best country on the face of the globe. At Villeneuve they separated, our party entering the steamer that was to bear them over Lake Leman.

"How did you like him, Minnie?" asked Walter, as the ex-president turned away.

"He is splendid!"

"A fine man, I think."

"How pleasant he was!"

"Yes, just as affable as if he had never held an office."

"I'll tell you, Walter."

"What will you tell?"

"If women are ever allowed to vote, I will vote for him. Hurrah!"

"You are not a woman."

"I shall be if I live."

"It will be a long time before women will vote."

"I don't think so, if what Mr. B. said in his lecture last winter is true."

"I remember it, but ——"

"No buts, Walter; the time will come."

"But how pale his wife was!"

"I noticed it."

"She is sick, and with her husband is staying here for health."

"She is dressed in mourning."

"Yes; don't you remember that dear little boy that was killed about the time Mr. Pierce became president?"

"No."

"He was killed near Andover, by a disaster on the railroad."

"She must feel sad."

"Yes; how would mother feel if one of us should be killed!"

"O, dear, don't talk of it."

"I can't help thinking about it sometimes, when we are in danger If we should die mother would feel so bad.

"Dear mother! precious mother!" sobbed Minnie, regardless of the people that were standing around.

"Come, children," said Mr. Percy, approaching at this moment, "the steamer will go soon. What, crying, Minnie?"

"No, pa, I was only thinking."

Chapter V.

LAKE LEMAN.

"HELVETIA! Father, the name of this steamer is Helvetia! What is she named for? What is the meaning of the word? Was Helvetia a man, a mountain, or a lake?" asked Minnie, all in one breath.

"Neither man, mountain, nor lake."

"Then it is a fancy name."

"No."

"What then?"

"Helvetia was the ancient name of Switzerland."

"That was it?"

"Yes."

"Then we are travelling among the modern Helvetians."

"Among the modern Helvetii, if you please."

"I don't see the difference."

"Perhaps you do not."

"But see, father, we are going — she has started."

"I see we are going. Now, children, you will

have a sail over one of the most beautiful lakes in the world, stopping as often as there is any thing to interest us; so remember and keep your eyes open."

The steamer went out upon the lake in fine style. The day was beautiful, and as a large awning was stretched over the deck, it was very pleasant sailing. But they had not gone far before Minnie espied something that at once arrested her attention.

"See," she said, "there are three trees growing right up out of the water."

"Where?" asked Walter.

"Right ahead! Don't you see?"

"Yes, I see now."

Mr. Percy now approached, and asked the children to take particular notice of the trees.

"What for?" asked Walter.

"Because there is an island beneath the surface, now concealed from view, but when the water is lower it is seen distinctly."

"What island, pa?"

"One that Byron writes about."

"O, I know — in the Prisoner of Chillon."

"Yes. Can you repeat what he says about the island, for the benefit of your sister?"

"I think I can."

"Well, do so."

Walter thought a moment, and then repeated these words : —

> "And then there was a little isle,
> Which in my very face did smile,
>   The only one in view :
> A small, green isle, — it seemed no more, —
> Scarce broader than my dungeon floor ;
> But in it there were three tall trees,
> And o'er it blew the mountain breeze,
> And by it there were waters flowing,
> And on it there were young flowers growing
>   Of gentle breath and hue."

" But where is the island, father ? " asked the girl.

" Under water, child."

" Overflowed ? "

" Yes, when Byron wrote, the lake was low, and the island in sight."

They had now swept on by the island, and were fast approaching one of the most interesting places on the lake.

" A castle, father," cried Walter.

" Yes, children."

They all looked forward, and saw the huge edifice standing just by the shore, with a water front, presenting a unique but pleasing object to the eye.

" Do we stop here, pa ? " asked Minnie.

"Yes, for an hour."

"Will you visit the castle?"

"Yes, we stop for that."

"What is the castle noted for?"

"Walter can tell you."

"Can you, bub?"

"Yes; it is noted for the imprisonment of Bonnivard."

"Bonaparte! Was he ever imprisoned here?"

"Not Bonaparte, but Bonnivard."

"Bonnivard? Who was he?"

"He was a patriot, who, for a vain endeavor to break the chain which was on his people, was brought to this place, and thrown into a dungeon."

The steamer had now reached the landing, and in a few minutes the party was at the castle. As they entered, Walter repeated what he had committed to memory long before:—

> "Chillon, thy prison is a holy place,
>   And thy sad floor an altar; for 'twas trod
> Until its very steps have left a trace
>   Worn, as if thy cold pavement were a sod,
> By Bonnivard! May none those marks efface!
>   For they appeal from tyranny to God."

They went down into the dungeon occupied

by Bonnivard. It is a dark arch, below the level of the lake, and a shiver passed over the frames of the children as they entered.

"I must know more of Bonnivard," said Minnie; "this place is yet a mystery."

"I think I can explain," said her father to her. "Bonnivard was prior of St. Victor, and he aroused the people of Geneva to rebel against the heartless Duke of Savoy. He was driven from his home, and here incarcerated."

"Are these his footmarks?"

"Yes."

"Why did he always walk in one place so as to wear the stone away?"

"Byron explains it. He puts into the mouth of the poor prisoner the following language:—

> "There are seven pillars of Gothic mould,
> In Chillon's dungeons, deep and cold;
> There are seven columns, massy and gray,
> Dim with a dull, imprisoned ray.
>
> * * * *
>
> And in each pillar there is a ring,
> And in each ring there is a chain;
> That iron is a cankering thing;
> For in these limbs its teeth remain,
> With marks that will not wear away
> Till I have done with this new day,
> Which now is painful to these eyes,
> Which have not seen the sun so rise
> For years.

* * * *

'They chained us each to a column stone;
And we were three — yet each alone;
We could not move a single pace;
We could not see each other's face."

" And was this the pillar to which he was chained ? "

" Yes."

" Did Bonnivard die here ? "

" No."

" He says, ' We were three ! ' "

" Yes, two brothers were imprisoned with him."

" Did they die here ? "

" They did."

" Please tell me the circumstances — do."

" The two brothers, who were shut up with Bonnivard in this cell, pined and died. He laid their limbs to rest, but no one came to bury them; and for two years the only companions the good man had were the dead forms of his two loved relatives."

" Has Byron said any thing about either of these brothers ? "

" He has; perhaps Walter knows what he said."

" Yes, sir, I do," answered Walter. " I have read that so much that I can repeat it."

"Well, repeat it."

Walter repeated the following: —

> "I said my nearer brother pined;
> I said his mighty heart declined;
> He loathed and put away his food;
> It was not that 'twas coarse and rude,
> For we were used to hunters' fare,
> And for the like had little care.
>
> * * * *
>
> My brother's soul was of that mould
> Which in a palace had grown cold,
> Had his free breathing been denied
> The range of the steep mountain's side;
> But why delay the truth? — he died!"

"How did Bonnivard escape?" asked Minnie.

"He remained here until the Duke of Savoy lost his power, and Geneva was free. Then the patriots came and opened his dungeon."

"Was he glad?"

"What do you think?"

"O, I know he must have been glad."

"What do you think the first question he asked was?"

"I do not know."

"Guess."

"Perhaps about his parents."

"No."

"About his property."

"No."

"About where he should go."

"No."

"Then I cannot guess; what was it?"

"Is Geneva free?"

"What did they tell him?"

"That Geneva was free."

When they had looked about the dungeons long enough, the children were taken to see a beam to which they were told two hundred Jews had been hung.

"Two hundred of them?" asked Minnie.

"Yes," said Mr. Tenant.

"It could not be. The beam would not hold so many."

"They were not hung at once, but when one lot was hung, another lot was brought."

"What did they do with them after they were dead?"

"Threw them into the lake."

"O, how awful!"

"A hundred years ago the world was very cruel."

"I should think it was, from what we see of instruments of torture and prisons. The trap doors, dark passages, cold dungeons, and wicked-looking instruments, show us that this must once have been a fearful place."

As they again stepped on board the steamer, Walter said, —

"Byron was not truthful."

"Why do you say so?" asked his father.

"Because he says what is not true in relation to this lake."

"Ah, Byron's descriptions are regarded as very truthful and very beautiful."

"But look here; how deep is this water here?"

"Not very deep!"

"Well, hear what Byron says about it: —

> 'Lake Leman lies by Chillon's walls:
> A thousand feet in depth below
> Its massy waters meet and flow:
> Thus much the fathom line was sent,
> From Chillon's snow-white battlement.'"

"The poet took the liberty, so often used by verse-makers, of adding about seven hundred feet to the depth of the lake."

"Then it is only three hundred feet deep?"

"It is very much less than that in this vicinity."

"Why did not Byron state the fact?"

"Perhaps he supposed the lake to be a thousand feet in depth here beneath the castle walls, as it is that depth farther out."

"What place is this we are coming to?" asked Minnie, interrupting the conversation between Walter and her father.

"Vevay."

"How pretty it looks on the shore of the lake!"

"It is a very pleasant town."

The boat had now reached the landing, and Walter was about to leap on shore, when Mr. Percy, who did not wish to stop, cried to him,—

"Where are you going, my son?"

"On shore."

"No, no, I veto that."

"Don't you wish to stop here?"

"No."

Walter came back to the party, disappointed by the decision of his father; while Minnie asked,—

"What does *veto* mean? I hear you say, 'I veto that!' What does the word come from, and what does it mean?"

"It is Latin," replied her father, "and means 'I prohibit,' or 'I forbid.'"

"Then, when I hear that the governor of the state has vetoed a law, it means that he has prohibited it."

"You do not hear that the governor vetoes *laws*."

"I thought I did."

"No; he vetoes bills in the legislature."

"What is the difference between a bill and a law?"

"A bill is the draught before the legislature, upon which that body acts. It does not become a law until it has been passed by the House of Representatives and Senate, and signed by the governor."

"I see; the bill is a law just as an egg is a chicken."

"What do you mean by that?"

"Why, the bill is law unhatched."

They all laughed at Minnie's comparison; and while they were talking about these things, the steamer approached Lausanne.

"We shall certainly land here," said Walter.

"Yes, and remain a few days," replied his father.

Having disembarked they took an omnibus and rode to Hotel Gibbon. On the way they were supprised to find the streets full of people, and on every side signs of general rejoicing.

"What is it, father?" asked Walter.

"I do not know."

"They are celebrating our arrival, Walter," said Minnie.

"Hush, silly girl."

"Let us inquire," said Mr. Tenant; and he asked a gentleman who was in the omnibus, and received all the information he wished.

At every turn they were met with new demonstrations of joy. The people were in the midst of a great national festival. Arches spanned the streets; flags of various colors were suspended from the windows; mottoes, wreaths, and evergreens adorned the public and private buildings, and music was sounding in every street. The inhabitants, dressed in gala-day attire, filled the streets; cannon sounded from the neighboring heights; bells sent out a merry peal from every tower; and all the various signs of some great *fête* met them at every step they took.

"What does the gentleman say it is?" asked Minnie of Mr. Tenant, who had been conversing with the stranger in French.

"He says that the occasion of all this is the occurrence of the annual shooting match, which calls together multitudes from all parts of Switzerland. This festival is conducted with great enthusiasm. The people of the various cantons meet here, and spend a whole week in target shooting."

"Do they have prizes?"

"Yes; this gentleman says they have prizes of from five francs to five thousand francs awarded; and on this occasion it is estimated that forty thousand persons from abroad are in the city."

"Shall we see the shooting?"

"Certainly."

They reached the hotel, and took tea in the garden that was once the arbor in which Gibbon wrote the last page of his work, "The Decline and Fall of the Roman Empire." As they sat in the arbor, around a table spread with sumptuous taste, they heard the shouts of the citizens on one side, and saw the crescent-shaped lake, more than fifty miles long, stretched out on the other. As soon as tea was finished, the children persisted in going out to witness the festivities. They passed through streets decorated with flowers and festooned with flags, beneath arches bearing patriotic inscriptions. The shooting ground was laid out in an open square, enclosed on all sides by temporary buildings erected for the purpose. In front was a stupendous wooden arch, under which the masses enter the grounds. This arch was gayly decorated with flowers and festoons, giving it quite a fairy-like appearance. On one side, as they entered, was a long pile of buildings for the sale of fancy articles, such as visitors would wish to carry away with them to their distant homes. In another place was a monstrous eating-house, rough, but neat and comfortable, and which, some one said to them, would seat four thousand persons at once. The party went up and down among the rude tables, which were all occupied by women, all covered with flowers and wreaths, and men, some in military costume, and some in blouses; all chattering and merry as could be.

" Where are the shooters ? " asked Walter.

" Some of them are here, and others are at the sport, if we can judge by the sound of the rifles."

" Let us go and see."

They went out, and found in the background, opposite the entrance, was the building for the shooters. This was divided into different compartments, each having a clerk, who kept an account of the shots fired. The targets were in the rear, at a distance, as they were told, of four hundred and fifty feet. The Swiss carabine was employed by the marksmen, and they used it with wonderful accuracy.

After seeing the shooting for half an hour, they all wandered back to the centre, where something struck the eye of Minnie.

" What is that ? " she asked.

" I don't know," replied her father.

" Let us go and see," said Walter.

They soon found out what the building was— a small circular oratory, or glass house, a sort of crystal palace, in which were the prizes. The building being of glass, the prizes, which were hung up, could be seen. Here were purses, through which the shining gold was visible, silver and gold plate, splendid watches, musical instruments, and such like.

"Beautiful things," exclaimed Minnie.

"I should like to shoot," said Walter; "I think I could get a prize."

"I think you would find your prize a blank," answered his father.

"There is something out here," remarked Mr. Tenant.

"What is it?" asked both the children.

"We will go and see," replied Mr. Tenant.

They went out to the place, and found about two thousand people, men and women, dancing on the ground. The loose sand was disturbed, and the dust enveloped them, but did not seem to diminish their sport. The party wandered about the grounds until late in the evening, and then returned to the hotel. In the morning they went out again, and found things very much as they had seen them the night before. They also visited the cathedral, and some other places of interest, and having remained in Lausanne two days, took the steamer one afternoon for Geneva.

As they approached Morges, Walter noticed that a man was hoisting a flag, and he watched his movements. When the folds of the flag were thrown open, he saw that it was a huge black banner.

"What does that mean?" he asked of the gentlemen.

They could not tell.

"I know," cried Minnie. "We are on board a pirate."

"Phaw!"

"Pirates always carry a black flag."

"There are no pirates on this lake, Min."

"Well, what can it be?"

"I think we can find out," said Mr. Tenant; "you wait and I will go and ask some of these gentlemen. — I have found out," said he, a few minutes afterwards.

"What is it?" asked they all.

"Last Sabbath," he said, "this steamer ran into a pleasure yacht, and sunk her."

"On Sunday?" asked Walter.

"Yes."

"That is what comes of breaking the Sabbath. Does this steamer run on Sunday?"

"Yes."

"Were any lives lost?"

"Yes, seventeen."

"Who were they?"

"Mostly young ladies belonging to good families in the town."

"How sad!"

"Yes; the whole place is arrayed in mourning."

"Whose fault was it?"

"The blame is said to belong to the chief officer of this boat."

"Is he here now?"

"No; he is in prison, and in due time will be tried for the reckless waste of human life."

Thus conversing the steamer passed by the town of Rolle, which has a little island in its harbor, around which the steamer passes to get to the landing, and by Noyon, in which they saw a castle or tower, — which looked, as Walter said, as if it might have a history, — and arrived, just as the sun was setting, at Geneva, the city of Calvin.

Chapter VI.

HOME OF CALVIN AND LAND OF TELL.

THE party were on the alert the next morning for the "sack of Geneva," as Walter termed it; and at breakfast the plans were discussed.

"Children," said Mr. Percy, "do you know any thing about this city?"

"O, yes, father; we have studied it well in all the Guide Books," answered Walter.

"I know something of it, as you will see, when I become your cicerone, to lead you about," said Minnie.

"Where, then, do you want to go?"

"Every where," said they both.

"Where first?"

"To the house where Calvin lived," was Minnie's answer.

"I would like to have you go and see Dr. Merle d'Aubigne, to whom you have letters of introduction," said Walter.

"Well, as the carriage is ready, we will go out."

They rode first to St. Peter's Church, where

Calvin used to preach. The church has been altered, but the old canopy and pulpit still remain. Then they went to the house where Calvin used to live. It is situated in an obscure street. They entered the dark and dismal gateway, and knocked at the door of the room which was once the study of the reformer.

"Can it be possible," asked Walter, "that the great reformer ever lived here?"

"Yes. Up these very stairs, and into this cheerless study, the men who were associated with Calvin went, and held communion. Kindred spirits they were, engaged in a kindred cause. Here those volumes were written which have left such an indelible impress upon the world."

"But, father, how the people who live in this house stare at us!"

"They care nothing for Calvin, and hardly know who he was, and look upon those who come with reverence to survey the premises, very much as the barbarians of Italy look upon the artists who cross sea and land to study the works of the great masters."

Leaving the study, they went to the graveyard, where with Calvin sleep Sir Humphry Davy and many other noble men.

"Where is the monument?" asked Minnie. "I don't see it."

"There it is," answered her father.

"Where?"

"Why, just before you."

"I don't see."

And well the child might fail to see, in the humble monument to which she was pointed, the resting place of the greatest man of Geneva. Nothing but a square stone is over it, rising about a foot from the ground, on which are the simple letters, "J. C.," telling the traveller where he sleeps.

"Why is his grave so unhonored?" asked Walter of his father.

"It is not unhonored. Thousands of all creeds come to pay their tribute to his greatness."

"But why no better monument?"

"This plain stone was put there in accordance with his own dying injunction, in which he strictly forbade the erection of a costly monument."

From the graveyard they went to the library of Geneva, famous for its ancient manuscripts, and its antique books and pictures.

"We have not been where I most wish to go," said Walter, as they stood in the street.

"Where?"

"To see D'Aubigne."

"We will go there now."

They were soon at the gate of D'Aubigne's residence, and sending in their letters of introduction, (which documents Mr. Percy was always averse to using when it could be avoided,) were soon admitted. The great and good historian talked with the children, and interested them very much, while, in what they said about their own dear native land he also seemed much interested. On the following Sabbath, they heard him preach, and during their stay in Geneva received from him several little attentions.

On leaving Geneva they took steamer on the lake to Lausanne, where they took the cars for Yverdun, at which place they took a steamer on Lake Neufchatel. At a town of the same name with the lake, they left the steamer and took one much smaller, and which did not draw so much water, and pursued their way along a narrow river, some twenty miles long, but scarcely wide enough for the tiny steamer to cross. Walter thought he could leap ashore, so near the bank did they go. Often the keel was dragging on the muddy bottom; and when a passenger wanted to land, the steamer drew up to the side of the stream, and a plank was laid from the vessel to the shore, and the passenger walked over it, and the paddles began to move again.

They reached the little town of Biel, — which

the young reader will see by looking on a map of Switzerland, — and here occurred an incident which amused the children very much. They wished to go to Olten that night, and it was almost dark when they reached Biel. The depot was full of cars, several trains going out at once. Our party did not know which to take, and they tried to inquire. For a time they were unsuccessful. At length they found a conductor who understood a few words of English, and they appealed to him. They pointed at one train, and said, —

"Olten?"

"No," shaking his head.

They pointed to another train, and said, —

"Olten?"

Then they told him, the best way they could, that they wanted to go to Olten. He replied, pointing to where they were standing, —

"Stay put; I come."

They understood that he wished them to stay where they were until he came to them. But they saw one train after another leave the depot, until there was but one left.

"On board," cried Mr. Percy, and he threw his carpet bag into the car, and pushed in the children. Mr. Tenant followed; and on inquiry they found that they were on board the right train.

"Guess work is as good as any," said Walter.

"If you only guess right," added Minnie.

Late in the evening they reached Olten, and drove to the only hotel in the place, over the door of which Walter read, —

"Hotel Von Arx."

Perhaps the reader will be willing to inquire what the name of the hotel means; for, after the Percy children found out, they had a good laugh over it. From Olten they went on to Zurich, where the peace conferences were held after the late war in Italy, and a view of which we give. They also went up into the region made famous by the exploits of William Tell, and stopped one night in Altorf, near which place he was born. That evening, as they sat in their rooms in the little mean inn, Minnie asked her father to tell her about the hero.

"What hero?" he asked.

"Of course I mean William Tell."

"Well, he was born near here, in circumstances of poverty, his father being a peasant of Bürgeln. Tell was one of a number of men who formed a league to resist Austrian tyranny, and for this was proscribed and ill treated. At length the Austrian governor——"

"What was his name?"

"Gessler."

"I have read of him in our school books."

"Do you remember what he did that aroused the vengeance of the Swiss?"

"No, I believe I do not."

"Do you, Walter?"

"Yes, sir."

"What was it he did?"

"He put his cap on a pole, and had it carried through the streets, and required the people, when they saw it, to uncover their heads."

"O, yes," cried Minnie. "I know that, but I didn't think."

"Tell wouldn't uncover his head," added Mr. Percy.

"What did Gessler say to that?"

"He was indignant, and condemned Tell, for what he called insolence, to shoot at an apple on the head of his own son. Tell knew his dexterity with the arrow so well that he did not hesitate. The tyrant stood by and saw it done; and when the apple was carried away, and the lad left unharmed, he commended Tell. But just as he was doing so an arrow fell from beneath his frock.

"'What is this arrow for?' said Gessler.

"'To kill thee, if I had hit my son,' replied Tell.

SWISS CHEESEMAKER.

"'Well, miscreant, thou shalt yet suffer,' shouted the enraged governor.

"Tell was bound and taken in a boat upon Lake Lucerne, and while crossing a storm arose, and the boatman could not control the little craft, and asked Gessler if he would unbind Tell and let him assist. After a time the terrified wretch consented, and Tell took the oars."

"Was he very strong, father?" queried Minnie.

"He was."

"What did he do?"

"He took the oars, and in the fierceness of the storm turned the boat back towards the shore which they had so recently left."

"Did he reach it?"

"Yes, he reached the shore, and bringing the boat close to a rock, sprang out."

"Good!"

"Yes, it was a good leap for liberty."

"What then occurred?"

"When Gessler saw that Tell was about to escape, he ordered his minions to surround the rock."

"O, that is too bad."

"It was just right."

"How?"

"Because, when the soldiers were gathering

around the rock, headed by the tyrant himself, Tell let fly an arrow and shot him."

"Did he?"

"Yes; and the soldiers, many of whom sympathized with Tell, who had just saved their lives, fled."

"What followed?"

"A general insurrection, and a long war, that did not end until long after Tell was dead."

"How did he die?"

"He lost his life in an inundation."

"I thought," said Walter, "that he lost his life at the battle of Morgarten."

"No, you are mistaken there."

"Do the Swiss people think much of Tell?" asked Minnie.

"Yes."

"Have they reared any monuments to his memory?"

"Yes; after his death a chapel was erected on the rock where he sprang ashore, and for many years the people in large numbers used to visit the spot."

"What became of the little boy who had the apple on his head?"

"I think there is no information on that subject."

"Are the Swiss a very brave people?"

"Yes; their history is full of heroic deeds."

"Mr. Tenant says there is something in the wildness of the scenery to inspire heroism."

"It is so. A people living in a cold, severe, mountainous region are apt to be more hardy and vigorous than in milder climes. The Italians, you noticed, were enervated, and often cowardly. These Swiss peasants brave all sorts of danger. New England owes much to her climate for the stern, rugged virtues of her people."

"How do the people of Switzerland support themselves?" asked Walter. "I do not see."

"Many of them live on very small means. If you could know how little it takes to support a Swiss family among the mountains, you would be surprised."

"How is it, father?"

"A large family of children will be supported by a few goats."

"It must be small support.

"And yet they are as contented as we, who have thousands of dollars."

"They have many cows here, I see."

"Yes; some of the cows are very fine, and from their milk an excellent cheese is made."

"What do the cows all have little tinkling bells around their necks for?"

"It is partly custom, and partly to find them more easily when they wander."

"I am told by Mr. Tenant that the cheeses are made here so that they are kept a long time."

"I believe so. It has been said that M. Ramond boasted of having eaten some, at the table of the *curé* of Lauterbrunnen, which had been made sixty years. And it is said that ' the *curé* of Ferden, wishing to present a visitor with what he deemed a delicacy, had a cheese served up which he said was of the venerable age of a hundred years.'"

"Do you suppose that true?"

"No; I think it an exaggeration."

"Do any Swiss cheeses go to America?"

"O, yes."

"Have we ever had any at our table?"

"Yes, occasionally."

"What is it called?"

"Schabzieger cheese."

"If, when we get home, you ever have any, let me know."

"If I think of it I will."

"O, dear, I am tired."

"It is time for you to go to bed. Take sis

and show her to her room, and then retire yourself. Where is Minnie?"

"She is asleep. Wake up, Min."

"What do you want?" asked the girl, yawning.

"I want you to go to bed."

"I am ready. Good night, father. Good night, Mr. Tenant."

"Good night," said each of the gentlemen, and the children were gone.

Chapter VII.

MAMMOTH ORGAN.   CURIOUS CLOCK.

Before leaving Switzerland, the party visited Friburg, as Walter was very anxious to see the wonderful organ at that place. A party was made up, and the organist sat down to evoke the matchless melody, and the moment the sweet sounds began to roll out, conversation was suspended, and every one gave attention but Minnie.

"Who made this organ, bub?" she asked.

"Hush."

"How many stops has it?" she asked, after a moment's pause.

"Hush."

"What is he playing?" she queried.

"Don't trouble me now," answered Walter, lost in the dreamy gush of sounds.

The organist was playing that famous piece of music which is so well adapted to bring out the wonderful power and excellence of the instrument — the Storm. First are heard the low, plaintive notes, as if the wind was sighing on the distant mountains; then it approaches, swelling louder and longer, gathering force and strength, until it sweeps on with driving rain and rattling thunder; and a person listening for the first time almost imagines himself in the midst of leaping avalanches, destructive tornadoes, and howling tempests.

"What do you think of that, Min?" asked Walter, afterwards.

"Terrific music!"

"Wasn't it, though?"

"Yes; I was almost frightened."

"I was not frightened, for I had read of this noble instrument. It has been frequently heard by travellers, who have been nervously affected by it."

"Have they described it?"

"Yes; several of them have described the organ, and have stated the effect on themselves when they have heard it."

"Who has written?"

"Several persons; and among others I remember that Mrs. Harriet Beecher Stowe says that, while hearing this music, she felt herself lost in a snow storm, in winter, on the pass of Great St. Bernard."

"I wish I could feel so."

"Why?"

"Because I should have all the sensation of being lost, and none of the danger."

Mr. Tenant, overhearing this conversation, asked the children if they did not remember in the music one wild note running through the whole.

"Yes," said they both.

"Do you remember what Mrs. Stowe says about that?"

"I never read Mrs. Stowe's description," replied Minnie.

"Walter has; for was he not quoting it?"

"Yes, sir," replied the boy; "but I only remember what she says about being lost on St. Bernard. What does she say about the one wild note?"

"'One note there was,' she says, 'of strange, terrible clangor — bleak, dark, yet of lurid fire — that seemed to prolong itself through all the uproar like a note of doom, cutting its way to the heart like the call of the last archangel. I felt myself alone, lost in a boundless desert, beyond the abodes of men; and this was a call of terror — stern, savage, gloomy — the call as of fixed fate and absolute despair.'"

"I heard the discordant note," said Walter, "but it did not make me feel like that. It went piercing to my bones, but not so terribly as that."

ZURICH.

"When boys write journals and women make books, they exag——"

"Tut! tut! tut! Miss Pert."

"I was only telling——"

"An untruth."

"No, indeed; I would not do that."

"But here we are at the diligence office, so we will let the organ go now."

The next place at which the party stopped, after leaving Friburg, was Berne, where was a very wonderful clock, which at noon performs many remarkable feats; but as the children saw a more noted one afterwards, a description of this is omitted. From Berne they went on to Basle, a fine town of about fifty thousand inhabitants, where they had the first view of the Rhine.

"Where do you intend to stop?" asked Walter, as he saw his father looking over the list of hotels.

"I do not know. There are several good hotels."

"What are they?"

"One is *Les Trois Rois*."

"What a name!" shouted Minnie.

"I suppose it sounds curious to your ears."

"What does it mean?"

"The Three Kings."

"That is simple enough. What is another?"

"*La Couronne.*"

"Worse still! What is that?"

"The Crown."

"Is there another?"

"Yes; *La Cigogne.*"

"What is that?"

"The Stork."

"Any more?"

"Yes; Hotel *de Sauvage.*"

"I know what that is."

"Do you?"

"Yes; that is Hotel of the Indian."

"The 'Wild Man' is better."

"Let us take that, father."

"Why do you prefer that?"

"I know," said Walter.

"No you don't. What do you think?"

"Because you think Hotel Wild Man is a good place for a wild girl to stop at."

"That is too bad, Walter!" said Mr. Tenant, laughingly.

They allowed Minnie to have her choice, and the whole party spent a very pleasant day in Basle, visiting churches, and in looking about the town, which has more the appearance of a German than a Swiss city. Before leaving Basle, a discussion took place as to how they should go — whether by cars or steamer.

"There is nothing to see upon the Rhine for many miles," said Mr. Percy, "and I think we had better take the cars, stopping as we may think best."

"I agree with you," replied Mr. Tenant, "and of course it will please the children, if it pleases us."

"Yes, sir," answered Walter.

"I don't know about that," responded Minnie, much to the amusement of the rest.

They took the cars on the German side of the Rhine, and, crossing the river at Strasburg, entered that city just at night, and on the morrow went to the cathedral. The spire of this edifice was a source of much interest to the children, especially to Walter, who had a long list of high steeples, and heavy bells, and large buildings.

"This is four hundred and seventy-four feet high," remarked Walter.

"It looks like lace, just as the Antwerp steeple did," added Minnie.

"When was this built, father?" asked Walter.

"It was finished in 1318."

"Then it is very old."

"How old?" asked Minnie.

"You can calculate — can you not?"

"I suppose I can; but if you would tell me, it would be a shorter way of getting at it."

"And the shorter way of getting at it would be the means of your forgetting it before you get out of Strasburg."

"Let me calculate. It is now 1859, and if this was built in 1318, that number, substracted from the other, leaves five hundred and forty-one years as the age of this steeple."

"All right, though clumsily got at, sis."

"Come, children, let us go into the minster," said Mr. Percy; "it is near noon, and we must be sure to see the clock."

"The clock! What of that?" asked Minnie, as they went in.

"A remarkable piece of mechanism, as you will see."

They found others pressing in, and soon they were gathered where they could see the instrument, which is almost as large as a country cottage. It tells the time of day, calculates the changes of the seasons, tells all about the moon, when it quarters and fulls, is an explanation and illustration of the movements of the planets, and shows the times of eclipses and comets. It also plays several tunes, though not in the best style of art. As the children stood looking at it, a military company appeared on the face, marched, countermarched, performed various evolutions, and retired from the field. Then old father

Time, with his scythe, came out, and showed his withered face, six thousand years old.

The children were much pleased with this exhibition, but Mr. Tenant would not stay and see it through, as he said one view of the front of the edifice was worth a thousand clock exhibitions. And so, indeed, it is; for the front of the church is elegant and exquisite enough in its carvings to justify the declaration that the building " looks as if it was placed behind a rich open screen, or in a coil of woven stone."

They visited the monument of Guttenburg, who, it is claimed, originated printing in 1436, which is a very neat, tasteful thing. As they stood before it, Walter asked his father, —

" Was printing originated here ? "

" Three cities claim the honor."

" What ones ? "

" The Dutch say that Laurence Jansoen invented printing at Haarlem, in 1430. The people of Mentz claim that Guttenburg invented printing there."

" What about John Faust ? "

" He was connected with Guttenburg, but not until a few years later."

" I should like to have you give me some facts about the art of printing."

" I will, at some time. No art has done more

to elevate and bless the world. At first, printing was very rude. The old presses were cumbersome things, and it was very tedious to work them. But now the patent presses have made printing a wonder to the world. The huge cylinder press used by the London Times runs off twelve thousand sheets an hour, or two hundred a minute. Some time, when we are in the cars, and have leisure and opportunity to go into this, I will give you a history of the art of printing, from the beginning, and you will find it of much interest."

"I don't see how editors gather so much news, day after day."

"It is very laborious. No one who has never been connected with the press knows how much labor and talent it requires to give variety and value to a daily paper."

On the evening of the day of the visit of the party to Strasburg, Mr. Tenant said,—

"There is a dish here, peculiar to this city, — so it is said, — that I would like to taste."

"What is it?" asked his friend.

"It is called *Pâtés de fois gras*."

"What is it?"

"It is a dish made of the livers of geese."

"Ugh!" exclaimed Minnie.

"The creatures," continued Mr. Tenant, "are

shut up alone, and by various stuffing processes, the liver is made to attain an inordinate size."

Mr. Tenant said so much about the dish, that they all went out, and at an eating establishment found it, but by unanimous vote afterwards pronounced it not worth eating.

"Is there any thing more to see?" asked Mr. Tenant, the next morning. "If not, we had better start early on our way."

"I want to ride," replied Mr. Percy, "to Brand Strasse."

"Where is that?" asked both children.

"It is Fire Street."

"Fire Street!" said Walter; "why so called, and what is there?"

"It is called Fire Street because there two thousand Jews were burned."

"Burned! How?"

"In one vast bonfire."

"Terrible! What were they burned for?"

"They were accused of poisoning the wells and fountains."

"Did they do it?"

"No; the people were dying of the plague."

"When was it?"

"In 1348."

"What cruelties the people of these nations in Europe have been guilty of! I should be afraid the Lord would sweep them away with a flood."

"You remember that there is a promise that the world shall not be destroyed by water again, and the rainbow is God's beautiful emblem that his promise shall not fail."

"I should think, then, that the earth would open and swallow them up."

"It is because God is so merciful and kind that wicked nations are not destroyed. The great King bears with his rebellious subjects much longer than earthly monarchs would."

The company rode to the place where the bonfire was once kindled, and found every thing changed, of course, but were made sad by the painful memories of the dreadful deed. Then they crossed the river, and took cars again for a new field of study and reflection.

Chapter VIII.

THE GAMBLER'S PARADISE.

As they rode away from Strasburg, the conversation turned on what they had seen, and the clock was a prominent theme of interest. Minnie did not see how an instrument so intricate as that must be could be kept in running order, and her father told her that for many years it did not go at all. The maker of it died, and no one was able to repair it when it had once stopped. Mr. Tenant referred to several noted clocks — one at Berne, another at Versailles, and others at other places.

"There have been wonderful watches, as well as clocks, Minnie," said her father.

"I should think it would be harder to make a watch perform such feats, than a clock."

"Why so?"

"Because the machinery in one must be so much more delicate than in the other."

"Perhaps it is so; but I have read that 'during the reign of Catharine II., of Russia, an ingenious Russian peasant, named Kulubin, constructed a musical watch to perform a single chant. The machine was about the size of an egg, within which was a representation of the tomb of our Saviour, with the Roman sentinels on watch. On pressing a spring, the stone would be rolled from the tomb, the sentinels fall down, the angels appear, the holy women enter the sepulchre, and the same chant which is sung on Easter eve be accurately performed.'"

"I should like to have seen that watch; it must have been a curiosity."

"It was so, indeed."

"How did people measure time before they had clocks and watches?" asked Walter.

"By hour-glasses, sundials, and the clepsydra."

"What is the clepsydra?"

"It was an instrument used by the ancients for measuring time."

"Yes, so I supposed; but how?"

"By the gradual discharge of water from one vessel into another."

"A sort of water hour-glass."

"Exactly so."

"When were real clocks invented?"

"Some time in the thirteenth century."

"When were clocks put on steeples?"

"Some time in the fourteenth century."

"Were clocks invented before or after watches?"

"They were invented and used much earlier."

"Who invented watches?"

"One Peter Hele, in 1512."

"What kind of things were they?"

"Very rude and imperfect, compared with ours. The improvements have been made gradually."

"Were they always called *watches*?"

"No; they have been known by different names; at one time they were called *Nuremberg eggs*."

"Where are watches made most extensively?"

"In Switzerland; but in other countries are very extensive manufactures. But here we are at Baden-Baden," continued Mr. Percy.

"Why do you call it Baden-Baden?"

"It is so named to distinguish it from other Badens in Switzerland and in the vicinity of Vienna."

"How large is it?"

"It has about six thousand permanent inhabitants; but this number is swollen by thousands in the summer season."

"Is it a watering place?"

"Yes."

"Is it on a river?"

"Yes, on the Oss, a very insignificant stream. It is built on the slope of a hill which is crowned by a castle. The Margraves of Baden lived here for six hundred years."

"What government is it under?"

"Under the Grand Duke of Baden, who comes here to reside part of the year, but who has a castle on the Rhine, which I will point out to you when we sail down that river."

"See, we are stopping."

"Yes, we are there."

They left the cars, and went up into the town, which just at evening seemed very beautiful and serene, and Walter suggested at once that they should stop long enough to have a fine season of rest and recreation. This was agreed to by all.

The next day was spent in writing letters to friends at home, on the part of Walter; and in mending her clothes, and doing other necessary sewing, by Minnie. The two gentlemen strolled about the town, and obtained a very correct idea of the place, found out what would interest themselves and the children, and prepared for an easy, comfortable time for a week.

The succeeding day was the Sabbath, and it dawned in quiet loveliness.

"There is an English church here, Walter," said Mr. Tenant, as they sat at breakfast.

"A Church of England establishment, or a church in which the service is in English?" asked the boy.

"Both."

"Then we can spend a quiet Sabbath. I have not heard a sermon in English since I left Rome."

"You forget."

"Do I? I cannot recall any sermon in English that I have heard."

"Did not your father read one of Massillon's sermons last Sabbath?"

"O, yes; but that was not preaching, you know."

They went to the church, which was well filled with a quiet, attentive audience, where they heard a very interesting sermon. On their way from church, Mr. Percy said, —

"We shall not dine until five, and it is no use for us to go to our rooms."

"Well," returned Walter, "let us wander away from the town, and get into the forests, where we can be quiet."

"No, I have another purpose in view."

"What is it?"

"It will surprise you both."

"What can it be?" said Minnie to herself.

"I wish to take you to a gambling house."

"A gambling house!" cried both the children, in astonishment.

"Yes, the greatest gambling house in the world."

"But have you not told me never to enter a gambling place?" asked Walter.

"Yes."

"And will you take us to one?"

"Yes."

"Why, father, you must be crazy."

"No, I am perfectly sane."

"But what would mother say?"

"She would go with us, if she was here."

"What! my mother in a gambling place?"

"I mean just what I say."

"And on Sunday, too?"

"Yes, on Sunday."

"But how can you reconcile this with your principles?"

"I will tell you. Gambling is carried on here to a great extent, but differently from what you have conceived of it in America. Sunday is the day when the most money is made and lost. I want you to go, that the spectacle you see may be a sermon more eloquent than the one you have just heard. You will hear no noise; there will be no confusion; all will be orderly and quiet, and you will receive a lesson

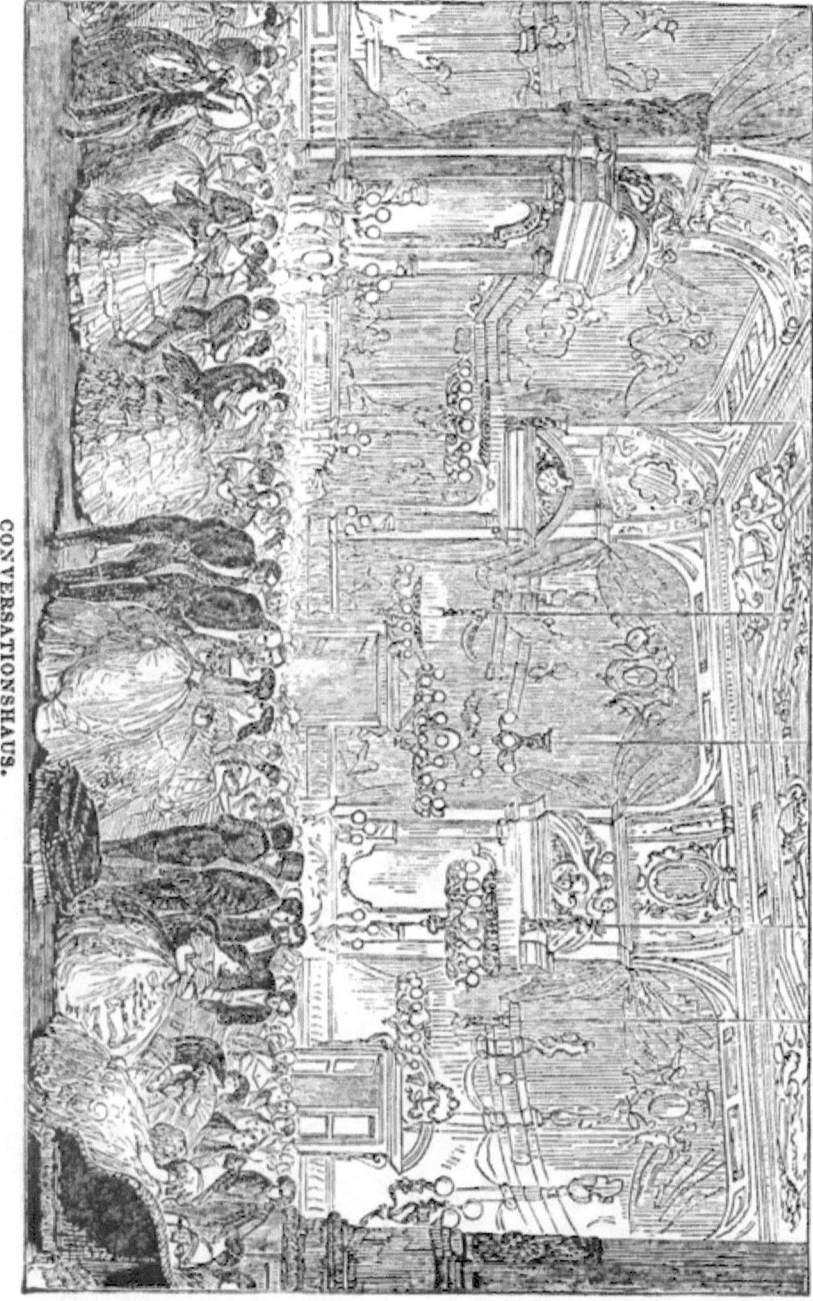
CONVERSATIONSHAUS.

which will impress your mind more seriously with the evils of gambling than any discourse our pastor ever preached at home. I shall take you there, just as a minister would draw a picture of the scene to deepen the effect of a discourse. If there was confusion, I should not go."

"I must, of course, submit to your judgment; but it does seem so strange!"

"You will see through it before we have made our visit out."

The party directed their way towards the centre of the town, to the seat of the pleasure seekers; and it being now afternoon, they found the unhallowed occupations in full tide of success. That the reader may understand what is now to be related, it will be necessary to describe the arrangement of things at Baden. The centre of pleasure is the *Conversationshaus*, a large building profusely decorated and arranged for gambling and balls. On a line with this edifice, which is an elegant structure, are other buildings for reading room, *café*, and various other purposes. In front is an open area for promenades. This area is surrounded with fancy stalls for the sale of all kinds of light articles, toys, and refreshments. The view of the interior of the *Conversationshaus*, occupied by many people, is on the preceding page.

This centre of pleasure draws thousands of people from all parts of Europe. So extensive are the gambling operations, that the house and grounds are rented for thirty thousand dollars per annum. Sunday is the liveliest day of the week, and a right-minded person can learn a moral lesson by looking in upon the scene, such as can be taught him nowhere else. Our party reached the grounds, and were soon in front of the *Conversationshaus*.

"This does not look like a gambling house," said Walter.

"It looks like a palace," said Minnie.

"Yet," replied Mr. Percy, "it is one of the worst gambling places on earth."

"Shall we go in, pa?" asked the little girl.

"Yes."

"Is there no danger?"

"None whatever."

They entered, and the children noticed that all the men took off their hats, as if they were entering a parlor or a church. They found themselves in a large room magnificently decorated. Gentlemen and ladies were walking about or lounging on cushioned seats. In anterooms the gambling was going on. Men and women were engaged in the various games. At one table the *rouge-et-noir* players were changing gold by the handful, and at another, *roulette* players were risking immense stakes. At the head of each table were men with little wooden rakes, with which they raked in or pushed away the gold. Minnie noticed that some of the most desperate gamblers were women, and a gentleman told her that some of the women were the wives of dukes and lords.

"How still it is!" whispered Minnie to her brother.

"Yes; no conversation above a whisper is allowed here."

"It does not appear like gambling."

"Not at all; I never saw any thing like it."

As they stood there, they noticed a young man come up to the table with a napoleon in his hand. He had a care-worn look and a very anxious face as he bent over the group of players.

"That is his last piece of gold," whispered Mr. Percy to Walter.

"How can you tell?"

"By his looks. Watch the result."

They had not long to watch. The young man waited until he deemed the propitious moment had come, and then threw his money on the table; and had he been playing for his soul, he could not have manifested more solicitude. A moment he gazed, and then saw his money swept from him. With a look of mingled desperation and woe he rushed away.

"Poor fellow!" said Mr. Tenant.

"Foolish fellow!" exclaimed Mr. Percy.

They saw a woman, with jewelled hands, approach and put down an immense sum with a careless look, and when she lost it all, she turned away, biting her lips with grief.

"The gambling is heavy and desperate," said Mr. Tenant.

"Yes," replied his friend, "and I think we have seen enough."

"I have, father. I would like to leave," said Walter.

"Not quite yet," coaxingly said Minnie; but her father was decided, and they all moved away.

"What effect has this had on your mind, Walter?" asked Mr. Tenant, as they were walking to the hotel."

"One that I shall never forget."

"What is it?"

"O, it is dreadful! The silence, the order, the awful look of interest and excitement! I would not be a gambler for all the world."

"I would not have you one for ten thousand worlds."

"If I had not always hated gambling, I think

I should now. The very splendor of the place makes it more dreadful."

"So all say who come here. The hushed breath, the solemn stillness, broken only by the clink of gold, make one afraid, as he looks on."

When they reached the hotel, Mr. Percy took his children into his room, and kneeling down, breathed out a prayer that his dear boy might be impressed with horror at the scene he had witnessed, and might profit by the sermon which had been preached him by vice itself.

The writer thinks that the party had better staid away from the *Conversationshaus* on the Sabbath, though doubtless the scene is impressive, and to a mind not yet debauched by crime, well calculated to restrain from vice; and it is introduced here to give a full idea of the wickedness of Baden.

The next morning they all arose early, and went up to see the Schloss, or old castle, in the crypts or vaults of which is an old secret tribunal of the middle ages. Murray throws a little light on the dark dens of cruelty. He says, that, " according to tradition, prisoners, bound fast in an arm chair, and blindfolded, were let down by a windlass into these dark, mysterious vaults and winding passages, excavated out of the solid rock on which the castle is founded. The dungeons were closed, not with doors of wood or iron, but with solid slabs of stone, turning upon pivots, and ingeniously fitted. Several of them still remain; they are nearly a foot thick, and weigh from twelve hundred to two thousand pounds. In one chamber, loftier than the rest, called the Rack Chamber, (*Folter-Kammer,*) the instrument of torture stood; a row of iron rings, forming a part of the apparatus, still remains in the vault. In a passage adjoining there is a well or pit in the floor, now boarded over, originally covered with a trap door. The prisoner upon whom doom had been passed, was led into this passage, and commanded to kiss an image of the Virgin, placed at the opposite end; but no sooner did his feet rest upon the trap door, than it gave way beneath his weight, and precipitated him to a great depth below, upon a machine composed of wheels armed with lancets, by which he was torn to pieces. The secret of this terrible dungeon remained unknown, until, as the story goes, several years after it had ceased to be used, a little dog fell through the trap door, and an attempt was made to rescue him, when the fragments of the ponderous wheels, set round with rusty knives, with portions of bones, rags, and torn garments adhering to them, were found."

Could the vaults and secret passages of all the castles of the old world tell their tales of guilt and crime, the heart of the world would cease to beat. Whether the above account is true or not, certain it is that these dungeons were once used for dreadful purposes. The children shuddered as they walked through them, and noted the memorials of cruelty.

Thus three or four days passed by, and the party were about to leave the town, when Mr. Tenant remarked,—

"We have had no baths since we have been here."

"O, yes, we have," cried all.

"I mean, we have not taken the bath at the place where it is given scientifically — for the health, you know."

"That is true, but as I am well, I shall not try it," answered Mr. Percy.

"I thought I should go out and try, and I hope some of you will go with me."

"I'll go," said Walter.

"Then I will remain at the hotel with Minnie, and have the trunks all packed by the time you return."

"All right," said Mr. Tenant; and they started.

They found the place where the baths were administered, and entered the building, a wet, dismal place, and met a man divested mostly of his clothing, who asked them if they wished baths.

"We do," replied Mr. Tenant.

"What kind?"

"I don't know; what kind have you?"

"Vapor bath — very good."

"Let me see what it is."

The man opened a box full of holes, and let the steam pour in, enough to take the flesh off the bones, and told the gentleman he was to pack himself into the box and shut himself in.

"That will parboil you," said Walter.

Mr. Tenant thought so too; so he asked what other baths they had. The man took him into a room, and showed him a place where hot water, almost boiling, came down upon the victim's body. Mr. Tenant shook his head.

"This is a water *torture* establishment," he said.

"Yes," replied the man, "a water-cure establishment."

"I cannot go that hot water, in the middle of summer."

"Will you have a bed bath?"

"A bed bath? What is that?"

"Come and see."

The man led him into another room, where

there were several beds arranged along by the wall, and began to explain how the bed bath was taken. The conversation caused some of the patients to bob up their heads, and Mr. Tenant perceived that two or three of them were women. He wanted no more, but turning back, gave the matter up in despair, and returned to the hotel, greatly amused with his adventure. When he related it to Mr. Percy and Minnie, they enjoyed it very much, and many a joke did they have at Mr. Tenant's expense.

"Farewell, most beautiful and most wicked place we have yet seen," exclaimed Walter, as, sitting in the cars, the town disappeared from view, and they were hurried onward with great rapidity. "Farewell, ye gambling fraternity, that use God's day for unhallowed purposes, and God's beautiful earth for scenes of sin."

"What are you mumbling to yourself, bub?" asked Minnie, who failed to hear a single word her brother said.

Walter did not reply.

Chapter IX.

HEIGHTS OF HEIDELBERG.

In the same car with our party was a monk, with whom Mr. Percy had a long conversation in the Latin language.

"Why do you converse in Latin, father?" asked Walter.

"Because this man does not understand English nor French."

"Then we can say what we will, and he will not understand us."

"He will know nothing of what you say, if you talk English; but I hope you would say nothing about him that you would not wish him to hear."

"O, certainly not. But what language does he speak?"

"He converses in Latin very fluently, but his vernacular is Italian."

"What do you mean by 'his vernacular'?" asked Minnie.

"The language of his native country."

"What kind of a monk is he?"

"A capuchin."

"There were many of that order in Rome; but I did not think to inquire why they are called capuchins? Why is it?"

"The capuchin monks are of the order of St. Francis. The name comes from the article he has upon his head."

"What is it?"

"A capuccio."

"And what is that? I don't get at it yet."

"That is a hood. You see he has it on his head. Sometimes he wears it thrown back upon his shoulders."

"What does the monk tell you? Does he give you any information such as would be valuable to a travelling gentleman and lady, like Walter and me?"

"No; we have been talking about the old relics of barbarism which you saw in the castle. He says that bad men must have used them. He appears to be a simple-hearted, kind man."

A ride of about three hours brought our travellers to Heidelberg. There were no incidents worth relating on the way, and the children declared it a dull route; but the moment they reached Heidelberg they were excited, and alive with interest.

"See the soldiers," exclaimed Minnie, as they were riding to the hotel.

"Where?" asked Walter.

"Why, all about you, with fatigue uniform on."

"I don't see them."

"Don't see them! are you blind, bub?"

"No, Min; but I don't see any soldiers."

"Well, there are dozens of them on the steps of that building there, and here come some on horseback; and — and they are all around."

"Those are not soldiers."

"What are they?"

"Students."

"Students in uniform!"

"Yes; the uniform is only a cap with red or gold band, indicating the class to which they belong, or the secret society with which they act."

"How do you know that?"

"Mr. Tenant tells me so."

Several students on horseback now came riding by, and Minnie waved her handkerchief to them, and in response they lifted their caps. They reached the hotel, dined, and then went up to see the castle, a prominent object of interest to the stranger. This castle stands on the heights back of the town, and combines the grandeur of the fortification with the beauty of the palace. They took a winding foot-path which led to the venerable edifice, and found it a hard but interesting walk, and stood upon the noble terrace, from which they had a grand view of the town nestling in the valley below, with the Neckar flowing through it.

"When was this castle built?" asked Walter of his father.

"In the middle ages. It was erected by different electors, at different periods, each one adding something to the extensive pile."

"What has ruined it, as we see?"

"It has been pillaged by war, set on fire, and struck by lightning."

The children stood on the terrace a long time, looking out upon the natural beauty of the landscape, and asking questions about the castle. Then they went all over the ruins, climbed up among the broken walls, and went into dark chambers, wondering as they went at the vastness of the edifice. They came to a part of the castle, which the guide, supposing they were English, showed them with much enthusiasm, as the English Palace.

"Why is it called the English Palace?" Walter asked.

"Because it was erected for an English princess," replied the cicerone.

"Who was she?"

"Elizabeth Stuart, granddaughter of Mary, Queen of Scots, who married the elector, Frederick V., and came here to dwell."

"Have you ever read any thing about Elizabeth Stuart?"

"No," said both the children. "What of her?"

"She wanted her husband to be King of Bohemia, the crown being offered to him."

"Did he decline it?"

"He did not wish to be king; but she said she would rather eat dry bread at a king's table, than be feasted at the board of an elector."

"Was her wish gratified?"

"Yes, she became queen, and came to want. At some time, when I have leisure, I will tell you the whole story. She saw the time when she could not get even dry bread to eat, without begging it."

Having looked about the castle, they went down into the vaults below. As they were descending, Minnie asked,—

"What are you taking us down here for?"

"To see a wine cask," replied Mr. Tenant.

"I don't want to see it."

"Don't say that, for you will be glad to see it when you reach the vaults."

"I have seen casks before, and I don't know why I should come down over these stones, and become so weary, just to see a cask."

"It is a different cask from any that you have ever seen."

"Well, lead on; it matters not to me whether it be dead kings or wine casks that I am to see."

"There it is," said the guide.

"O, monstrous!" exclaimed Minnie.

"Whew!" was Walter's comment.

These exclamations were drawn out by a sight of the famous Heidelberg Tun, as it is called, a mammoth wine cask, which is an object of interest to all who visit the castle.

"That is a monster!" said Mr. Percy.

"Have you the tape, father?" asked Walter.

"Yes."

"Let me take it and measure the cask."

The tun was lying on its side, and over it was a platform, on which dances are sometimes held. The lad, with his measuring tape, went up to the platform, and with the help of Minnie, who stood below, soon took the dimensions. The figures surprised them all; for, large as it seemed, the cask was larger than it at first appeared.

"How long do you find it to be, Walter?" asked his father.

"Thirty-six feet."

"How high is it, as it lies on the side?"

"Twenty-four feet."

"Measure the thickness of the staves, and see what that is."

"Eight inches thick," answered Walter, measuring the staves.

"When was this made, father?" asked the daughter.

"Long before you were born."

"That is not definite, pa."

"It was constructed in 1751."

"Then it is over a hundred years old."

"Yes."

"Has it ever been full of wine?"

"Yes, three times."

"When was it filled last?"

"In 1769."

"How much wine will it hold?"

"Eight hundred hogsheads."

"Whew!" was Walter's exclamation.

"How many bottles would that be?"

"Walter may calculate for you."

The lad inquired as to how he should go to work to make the estimate, and very soon replied,—

"It will hold about two hundred and eighty-three thousand and two hundred bottles."

When they had seen the tun, and were about to retire, the guide asked Minnie to open a door which was at hand. Unsuspectingly she did so, and out sprang a huge doll, which the guide told them was made by a servant of the elector, who had the tun built. The start given the child, by the appearance of the image, brought the rich blood to her cheeks, and made her little heart beat faster.

They did not forget to visit the library and museum of the castle; after which they went out and stood again upon the terrace, where for some time they admired the beauty of the prospect. As they looked on, Mr. Tenant remarked,—

"Heidelberg is said to be one of the most charming places in Europe, blending more natural beauties than almost any other city."

"I think it is beautiful; but I have seen places more beautiful," said Minnie.

"Other places," observed Mr. Tenant, "are often seen at a glance. Heidelberg must be studied. A vivacious Frenchman, Victor Hugo, has said that 'Heidelberg requires more than a visit — more than a summer's residence — nothing short, indeed, of a lifetime;' and one of our own matter-of-fact Americans adds, 'Heidelberg is one of the few German cities where I feel as if I could live and die, and be laid away to my lost repose, in perpetual content. It has every thing which a man of literary feeling could wish for — beauty of scenery, scholarly and artistic advantages, cultivated society, freedom and quiet.'"

"That is high praise."

"Certainly it is, but not unmerited."

At this point Mr. Percy advanced from a distant part of the terrace, and said, —

"I have a plan."

"What is it?" they all asked.

"Why, it is this: the hill rising behind the castle is the Königstuhl, and from the top one of the best views in the world is obtained. I propose that we go up and take the view."

"Agreed," said Walter.

"I will go," added Mr. Tenant, "but would like to stay all night and see the sun set, and rise again to-morrow. The view is said to be glorious."

"What say to that, children?" asked Mr. Percy.

"I would like to go," replied the boy.

"Of course I would," added the girl.

The guide was sent to the town for such articles as were needed for the night, and soon returned with the carpet bags, and a carriage, into which they all entered, and in three quarters of an hour were at the Kohlhof, a small inn on the hill. From this place they had a glorious view.

"There is Ebersteinberg Castle," said Mr. Tenant, looking through a glass.

"I see it," answered Walter.

"And there is a spire in the distance, as far off as I can see. I can just discern its outlines."

"In which direction?"

Walter pointed, and Mr. Tenant and the others were soon able to see it.

"What is it, guide?" some one asked.

"That is the spire of Strasburg Cathedral."

"Nonsense!" said Mr. Tenant.

"It is, sir," answered the guide, decidedly.

"But Strasburg is ninety miles away."

"And you see the steeple."

"Can it be so?"

"Certainly, sir."

While they were thus engaged heavy clouds rolled over the sun, and shut out what they had hoped to see — the sunset. Their disappointment was very great; and though the evening passed pleasantly, they were sorely tried. And with sunrise it was the same. The clouds obscured the king of day, and he came up unseen; and many were their regrets as they rode down.

"Walter is so disappointed that he has no scrap of poetry for the occasion," said Minnie.

"I am not always quoting poetry," answered the lad.

"Perhaps," remarked Mr. Tenant, "he has none appropriate to our disappointment."

"Yes, I have."

"O, what is it?"

"It has been in my mind all the morning. This is it:—

> 'Seven weary up-hill leagues we sped
>   The setting sun to see;
> Sullen and grim he went to bed;
>   Sullen and grim went we.
> Nine sleepless hours of night we passed
>   The rising sun to see;
> Sullen and grim he rose again;
>   Sullen and grim rose we.'"

"Pretty good, Walter, all but the 'seven leagues,' and the 'nine sleepless hours.' I have had five hours of delicious sleep," said Minnie.

"What kind of sleep is delicious sleep?"

"O, the kind of sleep you have when you are too weary to dream, and too quiet to wake."

They were now driving down hill at a rapid rate, and were soon in the streets below, on their way to the university. They met many of the students in the streets, and were courteously saluted as they passed along. They visited the

CASTLE OF HEIDELBERG.

numerous edifices, saw the library, and became acquainted with the officers.

A few days were spent in Heidelberg, most profitably and pleasantly, and the children made many acquaintances among the students. Minnie declared she would not believe the stories that are told about the duels fought by the students; but one of them, a boasting young fellow, assured her that he had been principal in seven, and showed her a scar which he had received in one of them.

"Barbarous!" replied the child.

He endeavored to defend the duelling practices of the students, but she would not hear him.

"Go away; I don't want to talk with a duellist."

And so the time in Heidelberg passed away.

"*En route* for — for somewhere," exclaimed Walter, as they left the beautiful town.

"For Frankfurt-on-the-Main," said Mr. Percy.

"There are two places I would like to have visited on our way down through this country."

"What places?" asked Minnie of her brother.

"One is Worms, where assembled the famous diet in 1521, when Luther appeared before the Emperor Charles V., to defend the heretical opinions he had embraced."

" What is a diet ? "

" A convention of ecclesiastics and princes to deliberate on grave matters."

" What was the other place you would like to have stopped at ? "

" Constance."

" Constance! I have heard of that city. What took place there ? "

" John Huss was burned there."

" O, yes, I remember. Tell me about it."

" Father tells me that the condemnation of Huss took place in a handsome Gothic cathedral, which now stands, nearly nine hundred years old. The spot where the martyr stood when the sentence of death was passed upon him, is pointed out to all who visit the place."

" I should like to see it."

" So should I. I wish we had thought of it, and persuaded father to stop there."

" What else is there ? "

" The old Dominican convent, now used for a nobler purpose, — as a cotton-printing establishment, — where Huss was imprisoned, is also seen. The council chamber where he was tried, his Bible, and many mementoes of cruelty still exist, and the stranger wanders through the streets, beholding at every turn something to remind him of the stern, iron reformer, whose burning took place in this city, on which his blood now rests. So says father."

"I wish we had stopped."

"Well, you know we could not stop every where, and as some places must be omitted, those might as well be left out as any."

"Frankfurt in sight!" said Mr. Percy.

"Hurrah!"

Chapter X.

FRANKFURT-ON-THE-MAIN.

THE party arrived at Frankfurt one day, and at the hotel where they took lodgings found several Americans, some of whom they knew. With them they passed a few days very pleasantly, and heard much news from home. Frankfurt is a town of seventy thousand inhabitants, the seat of the German diet, a quiet, opulent place, the residence of many men of note. The stranger passes his time quite pleasantly, and finds much to take up his attention.

"Frankfurt-on-the-Main?" said Minnie to herself. "I wonder why it is called so."

"Why do you think it is called so?" asked her father, who overheard her.

"I don't know, but I suppose."

"Well, what do you suppose?"

"I think I have heard of Frankfurt-on-the-Rhine, and I suppose this is Frankfurt-on-the-Main to distinguish it from that, and to show that it is not on the river, but on the main land."

Her father smiled.

"Isn't that right?"

"No."

"Why not?"

"Because you are as far out of the way as you can be."

"Well, why is it?"

"Because the town is on a river, it has the term 'on-the-*Main*,' applied to it."

"There seems to be a contradiction then."

"No, the river on which this town is situated, is the Main."

"O, ho!"

"You see now."

"Yes, pa; but I never knew it before, and I have always thought it was called so to distinguish it from a Frankfurt on the river."

"Remember what I have told you."

"I surely shall. But what is to be seen here? I don't like what I have seen."

"The Dom is here."

"The *Dom!* What is that?"

"The cathedral."

"The cathedral! Why do you call it the *Dom?*"

"The word *Dom* was applied, ages ago, to the pope; afterwards to lesser ecclesiastics, and at length to cathedrals."

"In Rome I heard cathedrals and large churches called 'Basilicas.'"

"Yes."

"Is the Dom worth seeing?"

"I can tell you better after I have seen it myself."

"How old is it?"

"It was commenced in 1415, and carried on for a century, and left unfinished."

"Is it still unfinished?"

"Yes."

"What is in it?"

"Some monuments, and pictures, and some other matters of interest."

"I have seen so many monuments and pictures that I don't care about seeing any more."

Afterwards, when they rode out to the Städel Museum, Minnie altered her mind about pictures. There were some there that she looked on with great interest. One in particular was greatly admired.

"What is that?" she asked her father, pointing to a large and striking picture in one of the rooms.

"That is the Trial of Huss before the Council of Constance."

"I have heard about his martyrdom, and would like to know all about him."

"What would you like to know?"

"The facts in his history."

"He was a Bohemian, born in 1373, and educated at the University of Prague."

"Yes, we were there."

"He was a preacher at the Bethlehem Chapel, as it was called, in Prague, and being made confessor to Queen Sophia, became very distinguished."

"Confessor! I thought he was a Protestant."

"While confessor to the queen he became acquainted with the writings of Wickliffe, the reformer."

"Before you go any further, pa, please tell me exactly what a confessor is."

"In the Romish church, auricular confession is practised. The penitent goes to the confessor, and tells him what sins he or she has committed. The kings and queens were accustomed in other days to have a particular confessor, and often the pope made the appointment. Huss was the confessor of this queen. He was to hear her penitential discourse, and absolve her."

"Yes, sir, that is what I thought it was."

"When Huss had read the writings of Wickliffe, he agreed with them, and began to preach them, and denounced image worship, confession, monastic life, and many other things practised by the church of Rome. Pope Alexander V. knew what was going on, and summoned Huss to Rome, but he would not go. The pope therefore instigated Shynko, the Archbishop of Prague, to persecute him. The preaching at Bethlehem chapel was abandoned, and at length Huss was summoned to appear before the council of Constance; and here you see him in the midst of the shaven-crowned ecclesiastics."

"How calm he looks!"

"Yes, he seems very self-possessed."

"And how bloodthirsty those priests look!"

"Yes, they are eager for his condemnation."

"How did the council decide?"

"That he was a heretic, and worthy of death."

"I should not have thought that Huss would have come to the council."

"He was promised protection and a safe return."

"By whom?"

"By Sigismund, the emperor."

"Why did he allow him to be condemned?"

"Because, like Pilate, he feared the people."

"How soon did they execute him?"

"A short time after his condemnation. He went to the stake with smiles at the rage of his enemies."

"Had he no friends?"

"Yes, very many friends; and after his death they rallied under the name of *Hussites*, and took dreadful vengeance on his murderers. Convents were burned, churches sacked, and monks murdered. The Bohemians formed in legions under the command of a knight, one John Ziska, and the whole land trembled beneath their march."

"How glad Huss would have been to have known all this!"

"No, he would have been very sorry."

"Sorry!"

"Yes; he was a kind man, and his pious heart would have been shocked at the deeds perpetrated by the Hussites. But come, we cannot spend any more time over this picture. Let us go."

The next day they visited the house in which Göthe was born. They saw his father's coat of arms over the door, and by paying a small sum were permitted to go into the room where the greatest German poet first saw the light. Minnie not seeming to know who Göthe was, Mr. Percy told her that he was a poet who was born in Frankfurt in 1749. His father was a doctor of law, and his son, inheriting his noble genius, rose to distinction as a poet and a statesman. His writings have been numerous, and his essays on the fine arts are much admired.

"I remember," said Walter, "to have heard a lecture on Göthe before our lyceum last winter."

"Yes, and that lecture was an admirable portraiture of the distinguished man who was born in this very room where we stand."

"Let is go to the next place," said Minnie. "I don't care about Göthe."

The next place was the house where the famous Rothschild family was cradled. The old house in which these eminent men, who have held the purse of nations, were born, situated in the Judengasse, or Jews Street, was an object of curiosity. Minnie had a hundred questions to ask about the wealthy Jews, and Mr. Percy gave her all the information he could, which indeed was very little. He told them that the father of the Rothschilds, Mayer Anselm, was born here in 1743; that he had five sons, who have grown immensely rich.

"Was the father rich?" asked Minnie.

"He was born poor, and was educated as a teacher, then became a small banker, and at length established a house which became known all over the world."

"What were the sons names?" asked Walter.

"Anselm, Solomon, Nathan, Charles, and James."

"Do they all live here?"

"No."

"Where do they live?"

"If they are all living now, Anselm is in this city; Solomon in Berlin, Nathan in London; Charles in Naples, and James in Paris."

"How large is their business?"

"It is quite impossible for me to tell."

"A single circumstance," added Mr. Tenant, "will show you, children, that it is enormous."

"What is it?"

"In a period of twelve years from 1810, these brothers supplied different European governments, in absolute loans and securities, with the immense sum of five hundred millions of dollars."

"What governments?"

"England, France, Prussia, Russia, Austria, Naples, and some other powers, were their creditors."

"Well, it is wonderful that such rich men came out of such a box as this!"

From the house of the Rothschilds they went to the house of Luther, where they saw his bust in front of the building, with a Latin inscription; and the children had many questions to ask about Luther. And though they had heard all the facts before, they were scarcely less interested than when first they heard them.

Thus two or three days were spent in Frankfurt, and then the party proceeded down the Rhine. On the morning of starting, Walter remarked, —

"This is my birthday, the 14th of August."

"Ah!" said Mr. Tenant; "how old are you?"

"Well, I hardly know. We have been about the country so much, and the months have come and gone so fast, that I must count up and see."

"What a boy! don't know how old he is!" cried Minnie.

"Yes, I do. I was eleven years and about eight months old when we left home, and so I must be thirteen now, as we have been away one year and about four months."

"You have grown since you left home, and have become much changed."

"How?"

"You look more manly, and you have more color in your cheeks."

"I am almost eleven," said Minnie, "and I guess mother will think we have both grown."

"She will think you have grown very ——."

"Bah! bah!" exclaimed Minnie, putting her hand over Walter's mouth.

"The carriage is ready to take us to the cars," said Mr. Percy, entering the room.

They were soon conveyed to the depot, and entering the cars, rode to Castel, where the steamer was to be taken on the Rhine. There is nothing at Castel worth the trouble of stopping for, and travellers hurry at once into the boat, or sit a while on the pier waiting for her to get up steam.

"There is a large city opposite us," remarked Walter, as they stood on the landing looking about.

"Yes," replied his father, without paying much attention to what the boy was saying.

"What is it?"

"Mayence, and it has thirty-six thousand inhabitants."

"What could be seen there?"

"Not much."

"Do you think we had better pass so large a city without seeing it?"

"I think so. What time we have remaining will be as well spent elsewhere. There is one monument, however, that I would like to have pointed out to your sister."

"What is it, pa?" shouted the child.

"Have you ever heard of Heinrich von Meissen."

"No, sir."

"Have you, Walter?"

"No, sir."

"Who was he?" asked Minnie, "and what of him?"

"He was an ecclesiastic, and a very great favorite with the ladies — he was called the ladies' minstrel."

"Poets are always favorites with the ladies," remarked Mr. Tenant.

"Not always," answered Minnie; "here is an exception. But about this ladies' poet, pa?"

"When he died, eight ladies supported his bier."

"What! carried it?"

"Yes."

"He must have been a favorite."

"They also poured wine, mingled with their tears, upon the coffin."

"Silly women."

"I think so too; but it shows how popular he was."

"What else is the city noted for?" asked Walter.

"St. Boniface once lived here."

"What saint was he?"

"An Englishman, who, in the eighth century, came into Germany, converted thousands of Germans to the Catholic faith, and for many years labored with much devotion as a real friend of the people."

A band now struck up a lively air, close by, and the children ran to hear the sweet strains that sounded wildly over the winding Rhine.

"What does that remind you of, Walter?" asked Minnie.

"I don't know."

"It reminds me of something."

"Of what?"

"Of home."

Chapter XI.

ON THE RHINE.

"FATHER, let me purchase the tickets," said Walter, as the time arrived for them to start.

"You may get your own, my son."

"Where shall I buy it for?"

"For Cologne."

So Walter went and purchased his ticket through to Cologne, and paid for it twenty-four francs; and soon all were on board, sailing down the river. The children went from one end of the boat to the other, looking at every thing they saw on the banks. They had not gone far when the boat began to lessen the speed, and soon a man went along the deck, shouting, —

"Wiesbaden! Wiesbaden!"

The vessel drew up to the landing, and about twenty persons came on board, and as many went ashore.

"Wiesbaden!" said Minnie to Walter; "I have heard of that place; I must find Mr. Tenant, and have him tell me what there is there."

Just then she espied that gentleman coming towards her, and she called to him,—

"I say, Mr. Tenant."

"What do you want, dear?"

"What is Wiesbaden famous for?"

"It is a watering place, like Baden."

"Why don't we stop there?"

"Because we saw gambling enough at Baden, and we should only have a repetition of the same scenes."

"Is there a great *Conversationshaus*, as at Baden?"

"A long building, called the *Kursaal*, which is devoted to dancing, gambling, and like things."

"Are there baths?"

"Yes."

"And fountains?"

"Yes; the most noted fountain is the Kochbrunnen."

"What is it?"

"A hot spring, which is used for drinking purposes by invalids, who go early in the morning to drink."

"How hot is the water?"

"The temperature is said to be one hundred and fifty-six degrees of Fahrenheit."

"Do they drink it hot?"

"Yes, as hot as they can bear it."

"How does it taste?"

"Like chicken broth, it is said."

"That must be curious water."

"It is very curious water, and I will read you a description of it by an English tourist, who came and tasted it."

"Who was he?"

"Sir Francis Head."

"What does he say?"

Mr. Tenant read as follows: "If I were to say that, while drinking it, one hears in one's ears the cackling of hens, and that one sees feathers flying before one's eyes, I should certainly greatly exaggerate; but when I declare that it exactly resembles very hot chicken broth, I only say what Dr. Grenville said, and what, in fact, every body says, and must say, respecting it, and certainly I do wonder why the common people should be at the inconvenience of making bad soup, when they can get much better from nature's great stock-pot, the Kochbrunnen of Wiesbaden. At all periods of the year, summer and winter, the temperature of this broth remains the same; and when one reflects that it has been bubbling out of the ground, and boiling over, in the very same state, certainly from the time of the Romans, and probably from the time of the flood, it is really astonishing what a most wonderful apparatus there must exist below, what an inexhaustible stock of provisions to insure such an everlasting supply of broth always formed of the same eight or ten ingredients, always salted to exactly the same degree, and always served up at exactly the same heat! One would think that some of the particles in the recipe would be exhausted: in short, to speak metaphorically, that the chickens would at last be boiled to rags, or that the fire would go out for want of coals; but the oftener one reflects on this sort of subjects, the oftener is the old-fashioned observation forced upon the mind, that let a man go where he will, Omnipotence is never from his view."

"O, I wish we had gone ashore. I would like to have tasted the chicken broth."

They had now shot by Wiesbaden, and were fast approaching Rüdesheim, where are several ruined castles. Mr. Percy pointed the children to the Brömserburg, close to the water, and related several legends connected with the quadrangular structure. He also pointed out the Brömserhof, a castle standing in the middle of the town, as if guarding it from foes.

"Is there a legend connected with that?" asked Walter.

"I presume there is, but I do not know what it is."

"Can you tell me, Mr. Tenant?" asked the lad.

"Yes, I believe I remember it. This castle was a long time the residence of the Brömser family. John Brömser was a noble knight, who in the crusade went to Palestine, where he was taken prisoner. Here he was confined for a long time, using in vain every means to escape. He had at home a beautiful daughter, whom he loved very much. While he lay in his dungeon he thought of her, and made a vow to God, that if he was delivered from the hands of the Saracens, he would devote that young, fair girl to the church."

"To the church?" queried Minnie.

"Yes, send her to a convent."

"Did he do so?"

"Let me tell the story. At length Brömser was liberated, and returned to Germany, remembering his vow with sorrow at every step he took. He loved his child; and now, as he was on his way to his ancient halls, he thought how desolate those halls would be without her who had been the light of his home and the pride of his life. But he had made a vow, and like that made by Jephthah, of which you have read in the Bible, it must be fulfilled. When he arrived, his daughter was the first to rush out and meet him, and when she saw how pale he was, she wept upon his bosom.

"Soon recovering herself, she led him into the castle, and told him how lonely she would have been during his absence, but for the presence of a young nobleman to whom she had given her heart, and promised her hand. When he heard that, he wept, and told her of the vow which he had made, and that she must soon prepare herself for a convent. She was at once filled with consternation, and began to plead with him.

"'Dear father, spare me!' she cried.

"'Gisela, I cannot.'

"'Father, you must; by all your love to me, you must.'

"'Gisela, I tell you I cannot.'

"'By all my love to Rudolph, you must.'

"But she pleaded in vain. His heart was fixed on the sacrifice she was to make, and nothing could move him."

"What a wretch!" responded Minnie.

"He was only acting in accordance with the spirit of his times. Parents then disposed of their children without consulting their wishes, or even asking their consent. We live in better days."

"Did he put her into a convent?"

"No."

"Why not, when he said he would?"

"Ah, that is the saddest part of it."

"Did she poison herself?"

"No; but finding all her entreaties disregarded, and resolved not to enter a convent, she ⸺"

"I don't blame her for that resolve."

"She went one wild night, and threw herself from the battlements into the waters below."

"O, dear! What did her lover do?"

"The legend does not say."

"What did her father do?"

"He was inconsolable, and wildly rushed up and down the river, shrieking his daughter's name: 'Gisela! Gisela! come to me, come to me!'

"But she did not come; her body floated down the Rhine, and was found by some fishermen, who carried it to the castle."

"Is there any more?"

"No; only that John Brömser never smiled again. The superstitious people who live along the river say that Gisela's beautiful form is sometimes seen moving up and down the banks, her hair dishevelled, and her white robes dripping with water."

"Do they believe that?"

"Yes."

"They must be superstitious."

"They say that her sad, mournful, dirge-like song, as it breaks forth full of tearful melody, is heard far and wide along the resounding shores, or echoing from cliff to cliff."

"Does any body live in the tower now?"

"Yes, some poor people occupy it as a residence, and they show the family furniture, and the chain with which the knight was bound in Palestine. They also have a picture which they tell you is a portrait of the beautiful Gisela."

While Mr. Tenant was relating this story, the steamer was going on, and old castles were seen on every side. Sometimes they were on the very shore of the river, and the waters lazily splashed against the wave-washed stones. Sometimes they were on steep cliffs and beetling crags, as if they were about to fall over of their own weight. Then they would be seen nestling in the forests, the trees of which seemed endeavoring to hide the majestic ruins, and conceal their decayed beauties. And then they were on the very hill tops, like giants stretching out their arms, sleepless sentinels, ever on guard. Some of these castles were in extensive ruin, some half decayed, and others occupied and in a tolerable state of preservation.

At one of the stopping places, a richly-dressed lady, accompanied by two gentlemen, came on board. Her hands were covered with rings, and her appearance indicated a person in good circumstances. At length the trio procured a table, and, taking out their cards, began to gamble. Money changed hands fast, and the attention of all on board was drawn to the transaction. Soon the lady took out some cigars from her reticule, and calling for a match, lighted the cigar, and began to smoke and puff away like a man.

"See her, Walter," exclaimed Minnie, in astonishment.

"Yes, I see her," answered the boy.

"A lady with a cigar in her mouth!"

"I never saw such a thing before. I have seen many women with pipes, but never saw one with a cigar."

"She is so elegantly dressed, too!"

"And how gracefully she does it! See how she rolls out those clouds of smoke."

And there, almost all day, this woman sat on the deck, with the cigar in her handsome mouth, and the cards in her jewelled hands, gambling, without one evidence of shame. But the children were so engrossed in the scenery of the river, that they did not pay much attention to her.

"Glorious!" would Minnie exclaim.

"Magnificent river! Royal Rhine!" would Walter respond.

"*Royal* Rhine, that is fitly worded, Walter," said Mr. Tenant.

"It is not original with me. Dr. J. Addison Alexander, in a graceful little poem, styles the river the 'royal Rhine.'"

"I never saw the poem."

"I have it in my scrap book."

"Get it and read it."

Walter took out his scrap book, and read the following apt lines, to which not only our party, but several English people who were near, listened with great attention: —

"I hail thee as an ancient friend,
 And as I cross thy line,
My democratic knee I bend,
 To greet thee, royal Rhine.

"The day and hour when last we met
 Come o'er me like a dream;
As then I saw, I see thee yet,
 Unchanging, changeful stream.

"The rush of waters o'er thy bed
 Distracts my laboring brain —
Forever dying, never dead,
 Buried, and born again.

"What is the secret of thy life?
 What holds thy channel fast

Amidst the elemental strife,
   The earthquake, and the blast?

"Why is it that the swollen tide,
   Which ever northward sweeps,
So warily on either side
   Its well-marked station keeps?

"Why dost thou not, old Rhine, at length
   Break thy ignoble chains,
And mustering all thy mighty strength,
   Submerge th' adjacent plains?

"Thou art a king among the streams,
   Thou river, deep and broad;
In regal pomp thy service gleams —
   To man, but not to God.

"Thy full, deep current, bold and proud,
   In his almighty view,
Is but the sprinkling of a cloud,
   A drop of morning dew.

"Though thou shouldst empty every rill,
   And drain the neighboring land,
Thy giant waters could not fill
   The hollow of his hand.

"The same almighty hand, that dri
   Thy current to the sea,
Can well control it when it strives
   And struggles to be free.

"And if at times that hand grows slack,
   And lets thee do thy worst,
He brings thee still at pleasure back,
   And rules thee as at first.

> "So, when I bend my stubborn knee,
>   To greet thee, royal Rhine,
> I render homage, not to thee,
>   But to thy Lord and mine."

"A pretty poem, the force of which one feels when floating on the bosom of this beautiful river; and I am glad you preserved the scrap, and put it in your book," said Mr. Percy.

"I have many beautiful things collected and preserved in my book. Whenever I see a scrap of prose or poetry which I like, I cut it out of the paper, and put it here."

"It is a good plan, my son. When we return home, I will procure for you an Index Rerum, — a book prepared with an index of subjects, — in which you can arrange all the pieces you have preserved."

"I have long wanted such a book as that. I saw one on the table of Mr. Falkner, one day, when he called me to him. As it lay open before me, I read, 'Let a young man, when he begins life, be in the habit of making an index to what he reads that is truly valuable, and at the age of thirty-five or forty, he has something of his own which no price could purchase. Many would think hundreds of dollars well spent, could they purchase what they have thrown away, and what each one might easily save.'"

"That is very true. It is the language of an eminent clergyman, who prepared that manual, and whose intercourse with men gives evidence that he has practised on his own theory."

"I shall value such a book."

"It cannot fail to do you a good service, if you use it properly."

"I wish you would get me one in England, and let me be using it on my voyage home."

"I will try to get one there."

"Thank you, sir."

Chapter XII.

BISHOP HATTO'S TOWER.

THE legends of one place were scarcely told before another castle came in sight, which had some curious traditions connected with it. The children went from one excitement to another, and all day long were asking questions and receiving answers. They made much sport of the curious tales told them of the towers on the river sides, some of them overgrown with ivy, and some of them looking as if they were all ready to tumble down on the heads of any who might enter them.

But in none of them were they more interested than in Bishop Hatto's Tower, near Bingen. The story of that old ruin was told by Mr. Tenant, who had read it somewhere, and who gave it to the children in a style that pleased them very much. The two gentlemen and their young charge were all standing together when Bingen came in sight, and the children saw the tower.

"What is it?" asked Walter.

"It is Bishop Hatto's Tower," replied Mr. Tenant.

"Who was he?"

"He was once Bishop of Mayence, and a very cruel man, the constant friend, favorite, and counsellor of the wicked Emperor Otho."

"Who was Emperor Otho?" asked Minnie.

"He was a haughty, selfish, cruel sovereign of Germany, born in 955, and had a father and son who bore the same title. Bishop Hatto was his friend, and led him into various wild and extravagant schemes, and incited him to many acts of crime and barbarity."

"What about the tower?"

"There is a very curious story connected with it."

"Let us hear it."

"The tradition is, that in a time of famine the bishop had large stores of grain in his barns at Mayence. For a time he sold it at most exorbitant prices, and as long as the money lasted the people had bread to eat. But so inordinate were the demands of the unprincipled owner, that at length the poor creatures had nothing to buy with. The bishop had all their money, and they were left in a starving condition. As hunger impelled them, they came to the residence of the bishop and begged for food, and as often as they came were sent empty away."

"What a cruel man!" said Minnie.

"Yes; any man who has grain, in a time of famine, and does not allow the starving people to feed on it, is himself unfit to live."

"And more unfit to die," suggested Mr. Percy.

"Very true; unfit for earth or heaven."

"Well, go on with the story," said the little girl.

"The bishop at length became wearied of the calls of the people, and determined to destroy them."

"Destroy them?"

"Yes."

"What for?"

"To get rid of their prayers for bread."

"And he a bishop!"

"Yes."

"I thought bishops were among the best of men."

"Some have been, and some are among the worst of creatures."

"Are they not ministers of religion?"

"Yes; but the German princes were often politicians and statesmen as well as priests; and at times the bishops became very corrupt men."

"Did such men preach?"

"No; they had vicars and assistants who attended to all the religion, while their superiors gave themselves up to political intrigues, dissipation, and crime."

"Well, did Bishop Hatto destroy the people?"

"Yes."

"How did he do it?"

"He sent out his servants in all directions, and told them that they could have as much grain as they wanted."

"O, he killed them with kindness, you mean."

"Let me tell you. He sent to these poor people, telling them that at a certain hour the barns would be open. Thus he enticed hundreds of them into one of his mammoth storehouses, and when the place was full, the monster caused the huge oaken doors to be closed, and the building set on fire."

"What, while they were inside?"

"Yes."

"What a monster!"

"Did they all burn?" asked Walter.

"Yes; so the tradition goes. When their dreadful cries fell on the air, and their shrieks of woe resounded far and wide, he laughed, and told his friends to hear the 'mice whistle.'"

"The mice whistle! What did he mean by that?"

"Simply, that the screams of these poor people were but the whistling of mice to him."

"That, you say, occurred at Mayence."

"The tradition says it did."

"What, then, has it to do with the tower."

"I will tell you. The tradition runs, that soon after this, the rats and mice began to make dreadful inroads upon the bishop. They devoured his grain; they gnawed at his doors; they found their way into his sleeping chamber; they tore his clothes; and at length fell upon his body. The bishop saw them every where; he was overrun, and his life was placed in jeopardy."

"Good! he ought to have been eaten up by them."

"So I say," added Walter.

"He found he could not stay in Mayence; if he did he would be devoured. So he thought of this castle on the Rhine, which belonged to him, and determined to remove here. He came, but was no sooner installed in his new home than the rats found him out, and began to throng around him. They swam the Rhine, climbed the hill, and scaled his castle walls."

"Good! good!"

"What, Min?" asked Walter.

"Why, that he should be tormented with rats."

"Not one," said Mr. Tenant, "could say that his fate was worse than he deserved."

"Did they eat him all up?"

"Yes; so the tradition says."

"Those are the rats for me!"

"The story goes, that they entered the castle, ate all the furniture, gnawned to pieces the valuable pictures, frightened off all the servants, and at length, falling on the bishop, actually devoured him."

"What an awful end!"

"Yes, if all this was true."

"But is the whole false?"

"No. There was such a bishop, and there was a famine in the land, and the bishop did decoy many into his barns, and burn them there; but that he was eaten by rats seems to want confirmation."

"He ought to have been."

"Perhaps so; however, it is said he died a horrid death, by a very loathsome disease."

"Have you never heard this story before, children?" asked their father.

"No, sir," said both.

"It has been wrought into a quaint poem, and I have it here."

"O, do read it."

"My eyes have already been tried to-day, and

I must be excused from reading. Here is the poem. Walter, you may read it."

Walter read in a clear, but low tone, the following verses : —

"The summer and autumn had been so wet,
That in winter the corn was growing yet;
'Twas a piteous sight to see all around
The grain lie rotting on the ground.

"Every day the starving poor
Crowded around Bishop Hatto's door,
For he had a plentiful last year's store;
And all the neighborhood could tell
His granaries were furnished well.

"At last Bishop Hatto appointed a day
To quiet the poor without delay;
He bade them to his great barn repair,
And they shall have food for the winter there.

"Rejoiced at such tidings, good to hear,
The poor folk flocked from far and near;
The great barn was full as it could hold
Of women and children, and young and old.

"Then, when he saw it could hold no more,
Bishop Hatto he made fast the door;
And while for mercy on Christ they call,
He set fire to the barn, and burned them all.

"'I' faith 'tis an excellent bonfire!' quoth he,
'And the country is greatly obliged to me,
For ridding it, in these times forlorn,
Of rats that only consume the corn.'

" So, then, to his palace returnéd he,
And he sat down to supper merrily,
And he slept that night like an innocent man;
But Bishop Hatto ne'er slept again.

" In the morning, as he entered the hall
Where his picture hung against the wall,
A sweat like death all o'er him came,
For the rats had eaten it out of the frame.

" As he looked there came a man from his farm;
He had a countenance white with alarm;
' My Lord, I opened your granaries this morn,
And the rats had eaten all your corn.'

" Another came running presently,
And he was pale as pale could be;
' Fly! my lord bishop, fly!' quoth he;
'Ten thousand rats are coming this way;
The Lord forgive you for yesterday!'

" ' I'll go to my tower on the Rhine,' replied he;
' 'Tis the safest place in Germany;
The walls are high, and the shores are steep,
And the stream is strong, and the water deep!'

" Bishop Hatto fearfully hastened away,
And he crossed the Rhine without delay,
And reached his tower, and barred with care
All the windows, doors, and loopholes there.

" He laid him down, and closed his eyes;
But soon a scream made him arise;
He started, and saw two eyes of flame
On his pillow, from whence the screaming came.

" He listened and looked; it was only the cat;
But the bishop he grew more fearful for that;

For she sat screaming, mad with fear,
At the army of rats that were drawing near.

" For they have swum over the river so deep,
And they have climbed the shores so steep,
And now by thousands up they crawl
To the holes and windows in the wall.

" Down on his knees the bishop fell,
And faster and faster his beads did he tell,
As louder and louder, drawing near,
The saw of their teeth without he could hear.

" And in at the windows, and in at the door,
And through the walls, by thousands they pour,
And down through the ceiling and up through the floor,
From the right and the left, from behind and before,
From within and without, from above and below;
And all at once to the bishop they go.

" They have whetted their teeth against the stones,
And now they pick the bishop's bones;
They gnawed the flesh from every limb,
For they were sent to do judgment on him."

As Walter finished the reading, various comments were made on the poem, and on the bishop, and all agreed that he deserved to be eaten by rats whether he was or not.

As they passed rapidly along, Mr. Percy pointed the children to the distant hills, which were all covered with vines, and remarked, —

" Those hill-sides are terraced, and if we were up among them we should find the vines covered with grapes."

"How long has wine been made?" asked Walter.

"I do not know; its origin dates back into very distant obscurity."

"I should like to know who made the first wine."

"The Greeks attributed the origin of wine to Bacchus, and the Egyptians to Osiris."

"They had it in the times of Noah," added Minnie.

"Yes," replied Mr. Percy, "they must have manufactured the article in the earliest ages of the world."

"Why don't we have wine manufactured extensively in our country?"

"The climate is too cold for the grapes."

"What is the latitude for wines?"

"Between thirty-five and fifty degrees."

"I have heard that much of the wine drank in our country is spurious."

"Yes, it is so; and the effect is observable in the rapid fall of the young men who begin to use it. The Bible says, 'Wine is a mocker,' and those who use the compounds called wine, which circulate among our young people, find it to be so."

"I wonder young men use it."

"I hope you will always wonder, and never

use it yourself. Strict abstinence is the only safe rule for a young man. If a boy begins to drink beer, or cider, or wine, he will soon go to more potent draughts, and is in constant danger of becoming a drunkard."

"I noticed," remarked Mr. Tenant, "that there is some kind of a festival at Bingen. The streets and houses are hung with banners."

"Have you any idea what it is?" asked Walter.

"No; the people are always having some kind of festivities, *fêtes*, or shows, boat races, horse races, cat races, or something of the kind."

"Cat races?"

"Yes."

"How can that be?"

"I read the other day that at Liege, in Belgium, on a recent occasion, a dozen cats were taken out a few miles from the town and let loose. The owner of the first cat that returned was to have a prize."

"Were they taken out in the daytime."

"No, they were carried out in bags, and emptied out just at midnight."

"What was the result?"

"The first cat came in in one hour, and the last not until some time after daylight, and a large number of persons came together to see the prize conferred."

" On the cat or its owner ? "

" Its owner."

" How very senseless that must be ! "

" About as senseless as many other things they have in Belgium, Holland, and Germany; about as senseless as some things we have at home."

" I have seen a statement recently that illustrates the power of ancient customs in these German towns," said Mr. Percy.

" What is it, father ? "

" There are two towns not far distant from where we are. One of them is Lambrekt, and the other is Deidesheim. It seems that the parish of Lambrekt have some privileges in the forests of Deidesheim, for which the former place obligated itself, in the middle ages, to send once a year, with certain formalities, to the latter town, a he goat. The animal must, on the third Whitsun holyday, be led by the youngest citizen of Lambrekt, by a cord, across the hills, and delivered at a certain place in Deidesheim before sunrise. The animal must be perfect, sound, and good-conditioned. The messenger, if he arrives in season, is to be well received, his wants attended to, and in the afternoon the goat is to be sold at public auction. The people of Lambrekt have often proposed to pay a sum of money instead of sending the goat; but to this the inhabitants of Deidesheim will not consent."

" Why not ? "

" Because they wish to have the conditions broken, so that the people of Lambrekt shall have no privileges in their forests."

" Well, what next ? "

" A few years ago the goat brought was in very bad condition, and the people of Deidesheim refused to receive him. A lawsuit between the two towns was the consequence, and this lawsuit has just been decided, after having lasted eight years."

" How was it decided ? "

" The legal tribunals decided in favor of the town of Lambrekt, on the ground that the goat was in good condition when he started, and ordered that this year eight goats be sent, one for every year since the suit commenced. The people of Lambrekt sent the goats, but unfortunately the young men who carried them were overtaken by a storm, and did not arrive until *after* sunrise."

" So they forfeited the conditions."

" Yes."

"What then occurred?"

"The people of Deidesheim assembled as usual on the morning of the 25th of May, in the gray of the morning, to receive the goats. But as the sun was about to rise, the excitement became intense, for the messengers had not appeared. The news flew abroad, the whole town came together, and when the sun arose, the whole place echoed with shouts of joy. The conditions were again broken, and the rights were forfeited."

"Why didn't the goats come?"

"They did, but too late."

"What delayed them?"

"They started from Lambrekt in season, but a storm overtook them, and they arrived just after the sun rose."

"What was done then?"

"The people of Deidesheim took the goats for the past seven years, but refused the last — the one for this year."

"Did the man carry him back?"

"No; all day long the animal stood tied to a post, unfed, and the messenger was received with scorn wherever he went."

"Will the people of Lambrekt give it up now?"

"No, another lawsuit will be the result."

"Well, that is a most curious circumstance."

"Yes; and it illustrates the old customs of the people of Central Europe."

"How old are these rights claimed by the town of Lambrekt?"

"I do not know, but probably hundreds of years."

"I should have supposed that these customs would have died out long ere this."

"No; they are as lasting as their towers and castles, and defy all modern innovations. There were many other curious customs, of which I will tell you at some time when we are at leisure."

"I will be sure to remember your promise."

"I see we are now approaching some other interesting places, which you must see and know about."

"Before you stop talking about Bingen, tell me about the emperor who was confined in the ruin called the Klopp. I read that there was such a prison here."

"Yes, my son, the Emperor Henry IV. was confined here."

"For what?"

"He was imprisoned by his son, who wished to reign in his stead."

"Tell us about it — will you, father?" asked Minnie.

"Henry IV. was born in 1050, and came to the throne when he was but five years old, and entered upon the administration of government at the age of fifteen. He at length became great and powerful, and by some means incurred the displeasure of Hildebrand, then reigning as pope, under the title of Gregory VII., who summoned him to Rome. Henry refused to go, and caused the ecclesiastics of his empire to renounce allegiance to the pope. Hildebrand excommunicated him; and so awed were the superstitious people, that they denounced the monarch. Henry soon found himself without friends, and was obliged to seek reconciliation with the pope."

"How did he do it?"

"He crossed the Alps to meet the pope, who was at the fortress of Canossa, with the Countess Matilda, one of his firm friends. Three days he was compelled to stand barefoot, and almost naked, at the door of the fortress, ere he could be admitted. At length he was allowed to see the pontiff, who granted him absolution."

"But how was he imprisoned here?"

"Various changes occurred with him after his reconciliation with Gregory. His eldest son, Conrad, rebelled against him, and endeavored to overturn his throne, but was defeated, and died in disgrace. The emperor then caused his second son, Henry, to be elected in his place, but made him take an oath that he would not disturb the empire while his father lived. This oath Henry V. disregarded, and seizing his father by stratagem, shut him up in the Klopp, from which he escaped, and died in disgrace at Liege."

" What an unnatural son ! "

" Yes; like Absalom, he wanted his father's throne."

" And got it."

" Yes."

Chapter XIII.

THE SEVEN SISTERS.

"RHEINSTEIN! That," said Mr. Percy, "is one of the restored ruins. It was once in a sad state of decay, but has been repaired and beautified."

"By whom?" asked Walter.

"By the Prince of Prussia, Frederick, who makes it a summer residence. When Berlin is sweltering in the sun, he brings his family here, and spends a few months in quiet leisure. The castle is fitted up with all the dreamy magnificence of feudal times, and resembles the old palaces of the knights of the middle ages."

"I wish we could go on shore at some of these interesting places. I don't like to be shooting down this river as fast as tide and steam can carry us."

"We cannot stop; you must see these castles from a distance, and let imagination do the rest."

"I see a road running along the edge of the river; is it a railroad?"

"No; a common road, on a shelf, as it were, just beneath the rock, and over the water. It is a sort of turnpike, and a toll was anciently levied on all Jews who passed over it — a tax. The owners of the road had little dogs trained to detect Jews, and when crowds of persons were going along, these dogs would leap upon the person of any Hebrew."

"Do you believe that?"

"That a toll was formerly taken of Jews we know, but the other part rests upon the uncertain statement of the guide books."

"Look," said Mr. Tenant; "see that tower rising above the houses."

"Yes," said Walter; "what is it, sir?"

"The village in front is Neider-Heimbach, and the castle is Heimburg. Just back of that is a ruin, once very famous as the head quarters of a robber clan. It is the castle of Sonneck."

"Is there any tradition connected with it?"

"Yes, it is said that this ruin was once a strong and handsome tower. Its owner was a man who had many vassals, and who sallied out and plundered the people wherever he could find them. In the middle ages, when each knight was a sovereign, and made the laws for the regulation of his own estates, they were often robbers."

"I thought," said Walter, "the knights were men of great honor."

"We should think many of them were very dishonorable, if they lived in our times. This knight was a brave, handsome man, who was feared for hundreds of miles around. One day, when riding alone near Mayence, he saw a young woman, standing on the bank of the river, looking over into the water. For a while she was unconscious of his presence; but as soon as she saw him, she fled to her servants, who were at a little distance waiting for her. The bold knight at once conceived the idea of carrying her away to his castle. So, hiding himself, he watched her, and soon saw her enter a noble castle. He understood very well that she was the daughter of a princely baron, and the betrothed of a young knight, a friend and favorite of the emperor. But this did not deter him from the execution of his purpose. He lingered around the castle until evening, and with the help of a trusty servant, seized the maiden, and mounting his horse, started down the river. But the shrieks of the captive alarmed the inhabitants of the castle, and soon the retainers of the baron, on fresh horses, were in pursuit. After ten miles of hard riding, five of the pursuers reached the side of the robber. With the maiden on his arm, he fought with desperation, and soon two of his foes were biting the dust in death. At length, finding the odds against him, and seeing his servant cut down at his side, the robber was obliged to release the girl to save his own life. He threw her from him, and with muttered curses, spurred his horse into a gallop, and left his pursuers in possession of his victim."

" He was a bold fellow."

" And bad as bold."

" Did he give up the idea of getting the girl?"

" No; some months afterwards, at the head of a large company of armed men, he attacked the castle of the baron, and after a desperate fight, bore away the maiden, and took her to Sonneck."

" What did her father do?"

" He went and found the young knight to whom his daughter was betrothed, and he went to his friend, the Emperor Rudolph, and demanded an army, which was granted. Placing himself at its head, the knight marched down the country and besieged the robber in his stronghold, and at length, finding a way into the tower, put the garrison to flight. The robber, seeing himself conquered, went into the chamber of the maiden, and told her that her lover had obtained entrance to the castle, and was on his way to her chamber, but would never see her alive. Just as her heart was beginning to beat with hope, he plunged a dagger into her bosom, and turned to meet the enraged knight, who was entering the room."

"What a wretch!"

"The knight sprang upon him and dashed him to the floor, and then turned to the maiden, who gave him one look of affection, and died in his arms."

"What did they do with the robber?"

"The soldiers took him and tore him limb from limb; and the young knight was so exasperated, that he set his men to pulling the tower down, and they did not leave it until it was a pile of ruins."

"When was that?"

"In the year 1282."

"What town is this that we are at now?"

"Lorch."

"What of it?"

"It is one of the oldest on the banks of the Rhine."

"What is there of interest about it?"

"Nothing, except a curious phenomenon called the 'Whisperthal.' It is a place where the north wind issues, which produces some curious sounds. The rocky ascent which you see is called the 'Devil's Ladder,' and the castle on the top is Nollingen."

Soon the steamer was opposite Bacharach. Mr. Tenant told the children that this was a place well worth seeing. It is a walled town, and has twelve towers, very substantially built, but having only three sides.

"Why is that?" asked Walter.

"The side of the towers towards the town is open, and it is supposed that they were built so, that an enemy securing one of them could not keep it, nor turn the batteries on the town. All exposed to the people in the streets, invaders would soon be destroyed."

"You said that the name of the town was Bach——"

"Bacharach."

"Curious name."

"Yes; there is a rock in the river below, called Bacchi Ara, or the Altar of Bacchus, and it is supposed the name of this town came from that."

"Shall we see the rock?"

"Yes."

"What about the castles?"

"You see it has old ruins."

"Yes, sir."

"The old fortress you see on the hill, behind

the town, is Stahleck. Just below is a church you cannot see, all in ruins now. It is the Church of St. Werner. Some time, ages ago, a boy, the son of Jewish parents, was murdered some distance below this."

" Murdered ? "

" Yes."

" What for ? How ? By whom ? "

" He was crucified by those who hated the Jews, and his body thrown into the Rhine. The story is, that the body of the murdered boy, instead of floating down with the current, which is very strong there, floated up to where we are. Here it was found and buried with great pomp, and this church built over the spot."

" Why do they let the church stay in ruins?"

" The faith in the story has died out. The Swedes destroyed the church in what is called the 'thirty years' war,' and it has never been restored."

" Look here ! " cried Minnie.

" What is it ? " asked Walter.

" A house in the middle of the river, and we are driving right against it."

" Mr. Tenant, what is it ? " asked the lad, looking forward.

" A castle."

" What one ? "

"The Pfalz."

"The *pf-álts!* What is that?" asked Minnie.

"The Pfalz means the Palatinate, and was built by Louis the Bavarian, as a toll house on the Rhine, and here a toll was taken for a long time."

"Was it an island, or were the foundations laid in the bed of the river?"

"It was an island — a rock in the river. When this fortress was built, the Countesses Palatine came here in times of sickness, to be away from the noise of the main land, and in time of war to be safer than on the shore. It has also been used as a prison, and down beneath the tide are dungeons deep and dark, and chambers filled with instruments of torture. If it is well garrisoned, it is a very strong defence, and could hardly be taken without a very great effort."

"What class of prisoners have been confined here?"

"State prisoners, or those imprisoned for political offences; and I have been told, though it is not probable, that there are rocky caverns beneath the Rhine, filled with human bones."

"You frighten me."

"You would be frightened to go in and see the dungeons."

"How fortunate we are to live in a better age, when such atrocities have ceased!"

"Cruelty is not yet banished from the world. If the prisons of Naples and Rome are ever opened, fearful histories will be revealed."

"Here we are down at Schönberg," said Mr. Percy, interrupting the conversation.

"And what new revelation does it bring?" asked Walter.

"It introduces us to the Seven Sisters."

"What do you mean by that?"

"Look over on the other side of the boat, and tell me what you see."

"Several rocks, against which we shall strike, unless the helmsman steers right."

"How many of them?"

"Seven."

"They are called the Seven Sisters."

"What have the seven rocks to do with the castle on shore?"

"I will tell you what the tradition is. It is said that in the castle lived seven beautiful maidens, and though they were besieged with lovers, they did not wish to marry."

"Hum!" said Minnie.

"The neighboring knights endeavored in every possible way to persuade them to enter the marriage state, but were unsuccessful. At length seven of them resolved to use force. In those days the laws were not so protective as now, and the ladies knew that resistance would be in vain, and to avert the danger, resolved to escape from the castle, and surrender it to the knights, rather than comply with their wishes. So they said to a deputation of the chivalrous men, that on a certain day they would be ready to meet them and select their husbands from the gentry of the neighborhood. The day came, and the knights in large numbers assembled. The ladies proposed that the choice be decided by lot, and professed a willingness to abide the issue. The lots being cast, the seven ugliest of the knights were selected. The ladies withdrew, as they said, to prepare for the bridal, which they insisted should take place at once. The seven knights waited long for their brides, and began to be impatient of their delay, when, on looking from the tower upon the river, they saw the seven maidens escaping in a boat, down the river. The gallant men rushed to the shore, and implored them to return; but they only answered the plea with derisive shouts and boisterous laughter. But the story goes that the gods of the river were angry with the fair fugitives, because they would not wed, as all beautiful maidens should do, and overturned their boat, and metamorphosed the seven sisters into seven rocks, which are now named for them."

" And that was the last of them, then."

" No."

" What! did they come to life again ? "

" No ; but the tradition runs that, while the morning star shines bright, they resume their original forms, and may be heard singing, —

> " 'The morning star shines from afar
> On mount and ruin gray ;
> Upon the shore we sing once more,
> Till glows the coming day ;
> Let no rude power disturb the hour,
> No rough wind shake the vine,
> Lurlei prolong our plaintive song,
> That swells above the Rhine.
> Thou morning star of hope to me,
> Thou star of hope to me!
>
> " 'O, may the train that fills yon plain,
> With merry hearts to-day,
> With joy and love, blessed from above
> Be innocent as gay.
> Pride once our own, we must atone,
> And ne'er remission know,
> Save when afar the morning star
> With holy light doth glow.
> Thou morning star of hope to me,
> Thou star of hope to me!' "

" That tradition is a silly one," said Minnie.

OBERWESEL.

THE SEVEN SISTERS. 199

"So I think; but travellers all hear it, and the handbooks give it with a great deal of gravity. Just below where the seven sisters, petrified and wave-washed, lay in the river, a round tower rose on the shore, and near it a fine town was seen, and Mr. Percy told the children the town was Oberwesel, and the tower one of the most noted on the Rhine. A view of this tower we give. The handsome edifice, seen on the hill back of the tower, is the Church of Our Lady, and is one of the finest specimens of Gothic architecture in Germany. Many of the inhabitants of the town were on the shore, as the steamer glided by, and some of them shouted and waved their hats, and the ladies on board the steamer waved their handkerchiefs in return. But the current is so rapid, and the steamer under such headway, that Oberwesel, the round tower, the Church of Our Lady, and the people on the shore, soon faded from sight.

Near Oberwesel, the steamer passed one of those huge rafts which are often seen on the Rhine. The rafts are composed of trees cut in the German forests, and which are of enormous size. They are chained together, and on some of them are little houses, with families; and often two or three hundred persons go down, in this way, on one float. Mr. Murray says, " The boatmen are often accompanied with their wives and families, spinning, knitting, tailoring, dressmaking; poultry, pigs and other animals are found on board, and several butchers are attached to the suite. A well-supplied boiler is at work night and day in the kitchen; the dinner hour is announced by a basket stuck upon a pole, at which signal the pilot gives the word of command, and the workmen run from all quarters to receive their messes. The provision carried on these voyages down the river is said, for one of the largest rafts, to be forty-five thousand pounds of bread, thirty thousand of fresh and dried meat, fifteen thousand pounds of butter, ten thousand pounds of cheese, fifty sacks of dried vegetables, five hundred tuns of beer, eight butts of wine, and other articles in proportion. At present the rafts are not so large as formerly; instead of being nine hundred feet, they are by law limited to seven hundred in length, and two hundred and fifty feet in breadth. They draw three feet of water. The smallest rafts require four hundred men to manage them. A single float is commonly the property of a great number of shareholders, and sometimes, at the end of the voyage, in Holland, brings one hundred and twenty-five thousand dollars. The annual amount of timber floated down this way, every year, and sold in Holland, is about eight hundred and fifty thousand dollars. The voyage down is sometimes six weeks, and sometimes, though rarely, it is completed in eight or ten days."

These facts Mr. Percy gave the children, as they were passing one of these immense floats, on which were hundreds of human beings.

Chapter XIV.

LURLEI, THE RIVER SIREN.

"LOOK out for the siren," said Mr. Tenant to the children.

"What is the siren?" asked Minnie.

"Why, children, here is the most dangerous part of the Rhine. Yonder you see the Lurlei Rock; near it is the Gewirr, a whirlpool, which makes this place very dangerous for small boats and rafts. There is also an echo to the rock, which has a very mysterious effect, as it bounds from cliff to cliff."

"But about the siren?"

"O, yes; there is a superstition that this rock is haunted by Lurlei, the beautiful river nymph, who lures boatmen from the safe places into her cataracts, where they are destroyed. She is supposed to sit on these brown cliffs and sing her witching songs."

"How absurd!"

"Yes, and yet many believe it, even now."

"The boatmen we have heard singing all day, and I should like to hear Lurlei."

"The boatmen are supposed by the tradition to come along unconscious of the presence of the sprite, singing as they come, while Lurlei charms them: —

Lurlei. Ah! come, boatmen, come to me.
Boatmen. We are boatmen, we are boatmen,
    On the bright and sunny Rhine,
And its clear and sparkling waters
    Fair and smooth around us shine.
Who enjoys so much pure pleasure
    As the dwellers on our stream,
When in merry rowing measure
    Splashing oars and bright eyes gleam?

Lurlei. Ah! come, boatmen, come to me.
Boatmen. We are boatmen, we are boatmen,
    And a merry life is ours;
Feathered spray and waters sparkle
    All around like fairy showers;
And the nymphs and fairies singing,
    As we glide along the shore,
Are new pleasures ever bringing,
    While we merrily ply the oar.

Lurlei. Ah! come, boatmen, come to me.
Boatmen. Hark! hark! the waves call us to join their wild
    chorus —
    They're murmuring sad at our unwonted stay;
The waters are dancing in madness before us,
    They sigh that we linger — we hasten away.
We go, O, we go, to deep, hidden recesses;
    We go to the shadowy ocean's dark caves,
Where amber and coral the sea-weed caresses —
    We hasten to join in the song of the waves.
      O Lurlei, we come."

"I declare, Mr. Tenant, you talk as earnestly as if you believed all this."

"I don't believe a word of it."

"Nor I," answered Minnie.

"Nor I," said Walter.

"And yet, many persons, living along these banks, do believe it. They say she has often lured the passing mariner into the cataracts at her feet, where she destroyed them. Many persons have perished here, and the ignorant people of the Rhine believe the beautiful enchantress is now sometimes seen on the top of the rock, singing and shining as of old. There are many who will say they have seen her, and heard her."

"O, fudge!" said Walter; "I am sick of these stories."

"I am not," answered Minnie; "please tell me about Lurlei."

"One tale that is told of her is this: the Elector Palatine had an only son, who was much beloved, not only by his father, but by all who knew him. He was hunting one day at the foot of the crags, when Lurlei saw him, and was just about to commence her charm song, and lure him to destruction, when she felt her bosom filled with love; and though she longed to bewitch and destroy the youth, this new emotion, which she had never felt before, caused her to remain silent, without discovering herself to him. For a long time after this nothing was seen or heard of her; but this young man was wonderfully prospered in whatever he undertook. The most troublesome horses were tamed by his voice; his feet always led him, too, in the chase, where there was the most game; and often, when he would lie down to rest, his ears were saluted with ravishing music from unknown sources. One day he was lost in the forest; the more he tried to find the way out, the more he became entangled, and the deeper he became involved. At length he climbed a high rock, and his eyes were at once fastened upon a female of surpassing beauty, who stood before him, her face half concealed by a transparent veil, and her person enveloped in drapery that but dimly concealed her voluptuous form. The young man, knowing who it was, and feeling his danger, closed his eyes for a moment, and when he opened them, he found himself at the gate of his father's castle. From that time he became possessed with the insane desire to see the lovely enchantress again. He communicated his wish and related his experience to his tutor, a wise old man, who endeavored with much earnestness to dissuade him from pursuing the matter further. The father of the young man, becoming possessed of the facts, obtained for his son a presentation at court, in hopes that absence would break up the dangerous delusion. But the day before he was to start from home, he went out with his tutor upon the Rhine, and turning his boat towards the Lurlei rock, approached nearer and nearer to the fatal influence. All at once, the tutor, who had been himself engaged in sketching some object in his scrap book, raised his eyes, and seeing where they were, exclaimed, 'My lord, are you blind! Do you not see Lurlei rock straight before you? For God and the Virgin's sake, turn!' But the young man steered on, and just at that moment Lurlei appeared upon the rock, and commenced her song. The boat, drawn by an invisible hand into the maelstrom, was overturned; the waves bore the tutor over to the opposite shore, but the young man had disappeared. The tutor returned to the castle, and requested a company of soldiers, that he might go and capture the enchantress, and save, if possible, the young man. He went, and reaching the crag, met the sprite, who said from behind her misty veil, —

"' Whom seek you, friend?'

"' The vile witch!' the tutor angrily replied.

"' Be not angry!' said Lurlei.

"' Where is our young master, vile one?'

"'Would you see him?'

"'Yes. Where is our beloved Edgar?'

"The sprite made no answer, but waved her hand; the mountain trembled, tempests rolled down the sky, the thunder rattled, and amid it all Lurlei stood radiant in her celestial beauty. The tutor was dumb; the sprite took off her necklace of coral, threw it into the sea, and all was calm again; then spreading her veil, and singing her songs, she descended to her watery caverns, and as the waters parted, the tutor saw his young master, with a face radiant with love, come and meet her. The legend supposes that the young Edgar, changed to a sprite, still lives, in unfading youth, with the beautiful Lurlei, in the coral caves, far down below. The boatmen of the river always mutter their prayers when they pass the spot."

"I don't believe any thing about these traditions," said Minnie; "but they certainly invest the river with interest."

"That is so; and when we search back and see what the tradition comes from, we generally find that it is some interesting fact."

"I have read," said Walter, "of the Grotto of Lurlei."

"Yes."

"What is that?"

"Simply a cave near the rock, where lives a hermit, who gets his living by discharging a pistol close to the rock."

"What for?"

"To awaken the echo, of which I told you."

"Is there any thing remarkable about the echo?"

"Yes; it repeats itself fifteen or twenty times."

"O, we must go ashore."

"We can't."

"We are losing much, by going down this river so rapidly."

"Perhaps we are, but we have no time to go in any other way."

"Children, we are coming to St. Goar," said Mr. Percy.

"What saint is that?"

"A town where many travellers leave the steamer, and where I should like to leave it."

"St. Goar — was he a saint?" asked Walter.

"Yes."

"Was this town named for him?"

"Yes."

"Please tell me something about it. I want to learn all I can."

"St. Goar was a hermit, who lived here in the seventh century, and who performed many miracles."

"I thought miracles were confined to the early ages."

"He pretended to perform them."

"What miracles?"

"He did several things which have become traditionary."

"What were they?"

"Among other things, he turned all the little birds on the church tower to birds of paradise."

"What else?"

"He hung his coat upon a sunbeam."

"Any thing more?"

"He threw up a piece of stone, and catching it in his hand as it descended, turned it to gold."

"How absurd that such stories should live!"

"And more strange, that even at this day they should find believers."

"The idea of hanging a coat upon a sunbeam, reminds me of the description given by a poet of the relics seen in Rome."

"What relics?"

"The poet enumerates them thus: —

> "'A ray, imprimis, of the star that shone
> To the wise men; a phial full of sounds,
> The musical chimes of the great bell that hung
> In Solomon's temple; and though last, not least,
> A feather from the angel Gabriel's wing,
> Dropped in the Virgin's chamber.'"

"Very good, Walter."

"But here we are coming to some other objects of interest."

"You must keep on the watch. The traditions we can have any time, but this is the only view of the river that will come into our tour."

They passed rapidly by the fortress of Rheinfels, once a nest for robbers, but blown up by the French in 1794. It is an extensive ruin, and the eye of the traveller lingers upon it, as the steamer darts down the river. Next they came to the twin towers of Sternberg and Liebenstein, which Mr. Tenant pointed out to the children.

"We see them," said Walter.

"I have a story about them."

"We will hear it," said Minnie.

"What is it?" asked Walter, who was tired of the ridiculous traditions.

"The towers are called 'The Brothers.' They were once owned and occupied by two brothers, Henrich and Conrad. These brothers, though loving each other very much, were entirely unlike. Henrich, the elder, was cool, calm, dispassionate, and venturous to a fault. Conrad, the younger, was wild, impetuous, but generous and amiable. Both were noble and elevated in their tastes, and pure in their lives. Unknown to each other, they both loved Hildegarde. The lady inclined to Conrad, and when the elder brother saw it, he nobly resolved to leave the field, and yield the prize to his younger and more fortunate relative. He buckled on the armor of the crusaders, and went to Palestine, where he was distinguished for his bravery. His frequent letters awakened in the bosom of Conrad a desire to go to Palestine, and to the great grief of Hildegarde, he set forth. The wars ended, and Henrich returned. By and by came tidings in no ways favorable to the constancy of the fickle Conrad, who, on parting, had vowed eternal fidelity to the maiden. At length he came back, not alone, but with a beautiful but frail Greek wife. Hildegarde's heart was broken, and Henrich, incensed beyond measure, challenged Conrad to fatal combat. When distances had been measured, and the weapons were grasped for life or death, Hildegarde rushed between them, and commanded them to desist. They obeyed, and coldly turned from each other. Hildegarde went into a convent. Henrich lived in seclusion at Leibenstein, and Conrad built the tower of Sternberg, and resided there. At length his Greek wife fled with another lover. Having spent his fortune, she deserted him. He then went, broken-hearted and penitent, to his brother, who forgave him, and the rest of their days they lived together at the castle of the elder."

"Here we are at a city — what is it, father?" inquired Walter.

"Coblentz."

Here the steamer stops an hour, and they all went on shore. They found Coblentz to be a strongly-fortified town of twenty-six thousand inhabitants. They went to several churches, rode through the streets, took a lunch, and drove back to the steamer.

"Can we not have time to go to the monument of General Marceau, before we go on board," asked Walter.

"Who is he, and what do you know about his monument?"

"I have read of him in history. In our school reader there is an account of his fall. He was killed at the battle of Altenkirchen."

"But how do you know about his monument?"

"Byron tells about it."

"What does he say?"

"I do not recollect the whole, but he begins thus: —

"'By Coblentz, on a rise of gentle ground,
There is a small and simple pyramid,
Crowning the summit of the verdant mound,'"

LURLEI, THE RIVER SIREN. 213

"Ah, yes, I remember the lines, but we have no time to visit the spot."

"Ding-dong, ding-dong, ding-dong," went the bell.

"All aboard! All aboard!" shouted Minnie, who was already on the deck.

"Ding-dong, ding-dong, ding-dong-dong."

"Hurry up, Walter," said Minnie.

"Hurry along, Mr. Percy," added Mr. Tenant.

They were soon on board, and the little steamer, with a monstrous lurch, shot out into the rapids and went leaping on.

When they were fairly out in the river, the bell rang again, and the passengers were called to dinner; and at the table, set on deck, they found a plain but ample meal. The children, however, did not wish to stay at the table. There were objects of interest on land, and they preferred gazing at them.

Chapter XV.

ROLANDSECK AND DRACHENFELS.

JUST below Coblentz are the towers of Rolandseck and Drachenfels, two ruins nearly opposite each other. The tradition connected with these towers interested the children. Rolandseck stands on a wild rock, and when viewed from the river, is a very interesting object. Drachenfels, or Dragon Rock, rises abruptly from the edge of the river, and is crowned with the tower, and a view of Cologne, twenty miles distant, is obtained from the top.

"Do you remember Byron's description of Drachenfels?" asked Mr. Tenant of Walter.

"No, sir."

"Have you ever read it, Minnie?"

"No, sir."

"Have you, friend Percy?"

"I have read it, but cannot repeat it."

"Can you, Mr. Tenant?" asked Walter.

"I don't know; my memory is growing poor, I find. Almost every such thing I committed to memory when a boy has left me now."

"Do try to give it to us."
"I will try.

  "'The castled crags of Drachenfels
     Frown o'er the wide and winding Rhine,
  Whose breast of waters broadly swells
     Between the banks which bear the vine;
  And hills all rich with blossomed trees,
     And fields which promise corn and wine,
  And scattered cities crowning these,
     Whose far white walls along them shine,
        Have strewed a scene which I could see
        With double joy wert *thou* with me.

  "'And peasant girls with deep blue eyes,
     And hands which offer early flowers,
  Walk smiling o'er this paradise;
     Above, the frequent feudal towers
  Through green leaves lift their walls of gray,
     And many a rock which steeply towers,
  And noble arch in proud decay,
     Look o'er this vale of vintage bowers;
        But one thing want these banks of Rhine —
        Thy gentle hand to clasp in mine!

  "'The river nobly foams and flows,
     The charm of this enchanted ground,
  And all its thousand turns disclose
     Some fresher beauty varying round.
  The haughtiest breast its wish might bound
     Through life to dwell delighted here;
  Nor could on earth a spot be found
     To nature and to me so dear,
        Could thy dear eyes, in following mine,
        Still sweeten more these banks of Rhine.

"But the story — the legend — you have not told us that," said Minnie.

"No; but I will do so. The old knight of Drachenfels, as the tradition goes, had a lovely daughter, who——"

"A lovely daughter always comes in."

"Who was beloved by young Roland, of Rolandseck, and who loved him in return. The father of the maiden saw with joy the attachment which was springing up between his dear child and Roland, for the latter was a fair and gallant young knight. But war called Roland from home, and he was absent many months. The war ended, and he returned, and a strange scene met his eye. The castle was being besieged by a robber knight, who had taken advantage of the temporary absence of the lord. Roland comprehended the whole at a single glance; he saw that the retainers of Drachenfels were falling, one by one, and that not a moment was to be lost. With the war cry of his ancient house, and with the few servants that accompanied him, he at once plunged into the thickest of the fight. The robber knight gave way, and his men began to flee, when a new foe appeared. It was the old lord himself. His visor was down, and Roland could not recognize him, and the old man, supposing Roland to be the robber, at once attacked him, and the father fell by the hand of the lover. When the maiden found that Roland had slain her sire, she yielded herself to hopeless grief, and bidding him adieu, went into a neighboring convent. Roland built this castle of Rolandseck, whence, from the windows, day by day, he could look out and see the convent that contained his heart's treasure. One day, as he kept his melancholy watch, he heard the convent bell toll, and soon after he saw a funeral procession pass out. His heart told him who was going to her grave. And ever after that he was accustomed to stand at the window and watch that grave, all day, all night. Often he would not leave it for his food, which his servants were obliged to bring to him. One day he was found dead at the window, the dead eyes open, and glaring on a distant grave."

Thus they went by one old ruin after another, hearing the tales of romance with which each is invested. These castles are now the haunts of robbers. The apartments once trod by beautiful women and brave knights are now trodden by thieves and assassins, though here and there one is seen in good preservation, and occupied by some noble family, who endeavor to keep up the ancient style and show.

Bonn is on the bank of the river, and has a

good cathedral, a fine university, and as the steamer passed it, the students were seen, in their peculiar style of dress, thronging the streets and lounging on the pier.

"Is the university a noted one?" asked Walter.

"Yes," answered his father.

"Can you tell me of any one who has graduated here?"

"Yes; Prince Albert, the husband of Queen Victoria, was once a student here."

"I should like to go on shore."

"It would be pleasant to do so, but time will not allow us to stop at these interesting places on the river. It would take weeks to travel from Mayence to Cologne, as leisurely as you would wish to do."

"How far are we from Cologne?"

"About a steamer trip of an hour."

"What shall we find between here and there?"

"Nothing of interest."

"Shall we have no more traditions?"

"No; the beauty of the Rhine, or rather its historic interest, lies between Mayence and Bonn."

"Then we can sit down and rest."

"Yes, if you desire to do so."

"I certainly do; my head and eyes ache badly."

So Walter sat down under the awning, and leaning his aching head against the rail, was soon sound asleep; and his father, knowing how weary he was, put a handkerchief so as to shade his face, and left him. Minnie ran about the steamer, asking questions of every person she could find who could talk English.

At length the towers and steeples of Cologne appeared in view. Walter was aroused from his troubled sleep, and the whole party began preparations for landing. After every thing was ready, and Mr. Percy stood with an opera glass in his hand, looking upon the distant city, and Mr. Tenant sat in a chair, with Minnie leaning on his shoulder, and Walter sitting on a box behind him, the latter said,—

"And now we are to bid adieu to the winding Rhine, the king of rivers."

"Yes," said Mr. Tenant; "and my eye was just resting on Childe Harold's adieu to this river, which is very beautiful, and every word of which I feel."

"Please read it."

"Well, draw up close to me, and I will do so."

Mr. Tenant then read the following verses in a low but distinct tone of voice, while the children, with eager interest, reached forward to hear every word:—

"On the banks of the majestic Rhine,
   There Harold gazes on a work divine,
   A blending of all beauties; streams and dells,
   Fruit, foliage, crag, wood, cornfield, mountain, vine,
   And chiefless castles breathing stern farewells
From gray but leafy walls, where ruin greenly dwells.

"And there they stand, as stands a lofty mind,
   Worn, but unstooping to the baser crowd,
   All tenantless, save to the crannying wind,
   Or holding dark communion with the cloud.
   There was a day when they were young and proud,
   Banners on high, and battles passed below;
   But they who fought are in a bloody shroud,
   And those which waved are shredless dust ere now,
And the bleak battlements shall bear no future blow.

"Beneath these battlements, within those walls,
   Power dwelt amidst her passions; in proud state
   Each robber chief upheld his arméd halls,
   Doing his evil will, nor less elate
   Than mightier heroes of a longer date.
   What want these outlaws conquerors should have
   But history's purchased page to call them great,
   A wider space and ornamented grave?
Their hopes were not less warm, their souls were full as brave

"In their baronial feuds and single fields,
   What deeds of prowess unrecorded died!
   And love, which lent a blazon to their shields,
   With emblems well devised by amorous pride,
   Through all the mail of iron hearts would glide;
   But still their flame was fierceness, and drew on
   Keen contest and destruction near allied,
   And many a tower for some fair mischief won
Saw the discolored Rhine beneath its ruin run.

ROLANDSECK AND DRACHENFELS.

"But thou, exulting and abounding river,
　Making thy waves a blessing as they flow
　Through banks whose beauty would endure forever,
　Could man but leave thy bright creation so,
　Nor its fair promise from the surface mow
　With the sharp scythe of conflict, — then to see
　Thy valley of sweet waters, were to know
　Earth paved like heaven; and to seem such to me,
Even now what wants thy stream? — that it should Lethe be.

"A thousand battles have assailed thy banks,
　But these and half their fame have passed away,
　And Slaughter heaped on high his weltering ranks;
　Their very graves are gone, and what are they?
　Thy tide washed down the blood of yesterday,
　And all was stainless, and on thy clear stream
　Glanced with its dancing light the sunny ray;
　But o'er the blackened memory's blighting dream,
Thy waves would vainly roll, all sweeping as they seem.

"Adieu to thee, fair Rhine! How long delighted
　The stranger fain would linger on his way!
　Thine is a scene alike where souls united
　Or lonely contemplation thus might stray;
　And could the tireless vultures cease to prey
　On self-condemning bosoms, it were here,
　Where nature, nor too sombre nor too gay,
　Wild, but not rude, awful, yet not austere,
Is to the mellow earth as autumn to the year.

"Adieu to thee again! a vain adieu!
　There can be no farewell to scene like thine:
　The mind is colored by thy every hue;
　And if reluctantly the eyes resign
　Their cherished gaze upon thee, lovely Rhine,

'Tis with the thankful glance of parting praise.
More mighty spots may rise, more glaring shine,
But none unite in one attaching maze
The brilliant, fair, and soft — the glories of old days.

"The negligently grand, the fruitful bloom
Of coming ripeness, the white city's sheen,
The rolling stream, the precipice's gloom,
The forest's growth, and Gothic walls between
The wild rocks shaped as they had turrets been,
In mockery of man's art; and these withal
A race of faces happy as the scene,
Whose fertile bounties here extend to all,
Still springing o'er thy banks, though empires near them fall."

As the last word was uttered, the steamer reached the landing, and the passengers began to rush ashore. The party waited until the rush was over, and then quietly went out of the steamer, and stood on the pier in the midst of a crowd of hackmen and porters, who were clamorous and uncivil in their importunity. Mr. Percy selected a sober, industrious-looking driver, and told him to take them all to Halländischer Hof; and soon they were at the door of that excellent hotel, which has two fronts, — one towards the city, and the other towards the royal Rhine.

Chapter XVI.

EAU DE COLOGNE.

THE hotel to which the party went in Cologne was full of people, there being much travelling at this season of the year. The front towards the town is not pleasant, Cologne being a very filthy city; but the river side of the house, commanding views up and down the Rhine and the villages on the opposite side of the river, is very fine. When Mr. Percy went in, he asked for apartments for himself and party. The servants were glad to see him, and ready to accommodate him, but took him up over two long flights of stairs into some dingy rooms on the town side of the house, where the view was blocked out by walls of brick and stone, and into which, from the streets below, came up the peculiar stench of the place. Mr. Percy told the servant that the rooms would not do for him — that the party must be accommodated on the river side of the house.

"That is impossible," said the servant.

"How impossible?"

"The apartments on the river side are all full."

"Is there no room any where?"

"None at all."

Mr. Percy was inclined to yield, and make the best of it; but Mr. Tenant, stepping up at that moment, said,—

"Then we must find another hotel."

"All in town are full, sir."

"We will try them and see." Then turning to Mr. Percy, he said, "We had better see what we can do; we shall get the plague if we stay here."

The party went down to the office, took their carpet bags, and were about going to another hotel, when the servant, with a polite bow, said,—

"Stop, gentlemen, and we will see what we can do for you."

"Ah," said Mr. Tenant, "that looks like it."

Soon the servant reappeared, and took them up into a fine room, twenty-five feet long and eighteen wide, with two ante-rooms, and said,—

"We have cleared this for you."

"This will do," replied Mr. Percy.

And well it might do. The room had three large windows opening upon the river; the ceiling was high, and the walls beautifully frescoed with Rhine scenery, and the children at once recognized some of the castles they had seen that day, and all the fixtures and articles of furniture were really very elegant.

"What made the servant tell you such a story as that, father?" asked Walter.

"I don't know; but as there is another boat to arrive to-night, and as river-side rooms are in great demand, I presume they are keeping the apartments that overlook the river for those who will not have those on the other side. Some travellers take their rooms in haste, without thinking of the disadvantages of a town-side view."

"Ah, I see through it now; but I should think he would be ashamed of himself, to tell a wicked lie about so small a matter."

"Well, we are finely convenienced. Napoleon could ask for no better apartments than we have furnished us here. We can sit this evening, and look up and down the Rhine, see the boats on the river, enjoy the refreshing breezes, and sleep soundly when we go to bed."

Cologne, or Köln, in the German, is a town of one hundred thousand inhabitants. It derives its name from the mother of Nero, who was born here, who called it Colonia Agrippina, and is a place of considerable note. The old Roman wall, and various relics of the past, are yet visible. It has figured largely on the pages of history. All the morning of the day on which our travellers arrived, Mr. Percy spent in giving the children historical reminiscences of the place, and they were very much interested by the recital.

The next morning they went out to see what was to be seen.

"Where shall we go first?" asked the lad.

"To the cathedral, of course," was the reply.

So they wended their way to this edifice, which, in some particulars, is most remarkable.

"This is the central object of interest here," said Mr. Percy to Walter, as they reached the cathedral.

"It is unfinished, I see."

"Yes; though it was begun in 1272, it is not yet completed.'

"Who built it?"

"Archbishop Conrad, of Hochsteden, was the master spirit in its erection, but the name of the architect is lost."

"How large is it?"

"Five hundred and eleven feet long, two hundred and thirty-one feet in breadth; the choir is one hundred and sixty-one feet high, and all the rest of the edifice, you see, is well proportioned. If the original plan of this church had been carried out, it would have been a more magnificent structure than the Cathedral of Milan, or St. Peter's at Rome."

"If the name of the architect was lost, how do they know what the original plans were?"

"Views of the edifice, as it was intended to be, are yet in existence."

"What is that thing I saw standing on one of the towers, when I entered?"

"What did it look like?"

"A derrick, I judged it to be."

"O, yes, I know. That is a crane that was put up here hundreds of years ago."

"Hundreds of years ago?"

"Yes; when the work on the towers was progressing it was used by the masons to get the stones up with. About one hundred years ago it was taken down; but on the very day when it was removed, a terrific thunder storm swept over the building, and the lightnings struck the tower where it had stood, and the superstitious people, seeing this, at once hoisted the crane to its place again."

"I see they are at work on it now."

"Yes; government is doing something to finish it, and money for the building is being collected by a society organized for the purpose."

"Who is architect of the edifice now?"

"Zwirner."

"How much money has been expended on it?"

"It is impossible to tell; but it must have reached millions of dollars."

"Whew!"

"And the architect estimates that it will cost at least three millions seven hundred and fifty thousand dollars."

"What beautiful windows!" exclaimed Minnie, the party having entered the cathedral.

"Very fine indeed," replied Mr. Percy; "they were a present from King Louis, of Bavaria."

"How many did he give?"

"Five."

"Have they any relics here?"

"Of course."

"What relics?"

"In a curiously wrought silver case behind the altar are said to be the bones of three kings of Cologne, who were the Magi who went to Bethlehem when Christ was born."

"Pho!"

"The people believe it, and the silver oratory where they are was once all covered over with precious stones and jewels."

"Where are they now?"

"Many of them have been taken away in times

of war; but the casket is still rich with them, some say to the amount of one million two hundred thousand dollars."

The party went to the altar, and saw the oratory, and many were the expressions of wonder at it. They also went into the sacristy, where they saw what purported to be a bone of Matthew the Evangelist, and some other relics.

" Look here, children," said their father.

" What is it ? "

" Look at this slab."

" What of it ? "

" Beneath it lies buried the heart of Mary of Medici."

" Who was she ? " asked Minnie.

" She was a weak, ambitious woman, wife of Henry IV. of France. After the death of her husband she reigned as regent, but administered the government so badly, and had so much trouble with her ministers, that she was banished from the kingdom, and died in great destitution in this city."

The party remained in the cathedral a long time wondering, and then rode to the church of St. Ursula, which is filled with bones, forming a most disgusting spectacle to one who does not sympathize with the veneration of relics."

" O father ! " exclaimed Minnie.

"What are these?" cried Walter, in astonishment.

"Bones — only dry bones, my son."

"Whose bones are they?"

"Of St. Ursula and eleven thousand virgins."

"Who was St. Ursula?"

"A traditionary character."

"Please explain all this — do, pa."

"This St. Ursula was, according to the Catholic legend, the daughter of a British king. With eleven thousand of her maidens she started from Britain towards Rome, which city she intended to visit on a pilgrimage. She performed her devotions in the holy city, and, under the escort of her lover, Conrad, and a number of valiant knights, commenced her return, and reached Cologne, where she was met by the Huns, and the whole expedition slaughtered. The bones, gathered by devout Catholics, have been deposited here in this church, and you see them set into the wall, and stacked up all about."

"Where are the bones of Ursula herself?"

"They are behind the altar; we will go and see."

They went, and saw the bones, and they also saw one of the jars which held the water which Christ turned into wine at Cana of Galilee, or what the priests said was one of them."

"Is there any foundation for this tradition?"

"I think not."

"Where, then, did these bones come from?"

"I cannot tell, but they were probably gathered for this purpose from all possible sources."

"What singular taste the people must have to cling to such a tradition, and keep up this disgusting show!" said Walter.

"The church is a great source of revenue, and thousands come here to see it. There is another church filled up in the same manner."

"Do not go to it."

"No; we shall not have time to see it. It is the Church of St. Geveon, and we are told it 'is lined with the bones of the Theban Legion of six thousand martyrs, slain, according to the legend told here, either on this spot or at Xanten, in the time of the persecution of Diocletian.'"

During the day they went to several churches; among which were Santa Maria, in Capitolio, so called because it stands where an old Roman capitol used to stand, and which, as Hope says, "internally resembles a Greek church, and is, in fact, a counterpart of one existing among the ruins of Seleucia, since round its semicircular absides and east end run internally semicircular rows of columns supporting round arches;" the Apostles' Church, an old structure of eight hundred years' standing; the Jesuit Church, which contains many relics, among the most interesting of which are the crosier of Francis Xavier, and the rosary of Ignatius Loyola; and several others of great beauty, and containing some fine paintings.

As they went about the streets, they were surprised at the foul stench that seemed to arise on every side, and fill the air with pestilence.

"It's too bad!" exclaimed Minnie.

"What is too bad, sis?" asked her brother.

"That so fine a city should be kept in such a filthy condition."

"The houses are drained into the streets, and all visitors are struck with the filthiness of the town," said Mr. Tenant. "The stench has been commemorated in prose and poetry."

"Poetry?" asked Walter.

"Yes; some of the sharpest and most cutting things ever put into verse have been written about this city, which should be one of the best drained and cleanest cities on the Rhine. The sarcastic Coleridge exclaims, —

> "Ye nymphs, who reign o'er sewers and sinks,
> The River Rhine, it is well known,
> Doth wash your city of Cologne:
> But tell me, nymphs, what power divine
> Shall henceforth wash the River Rhine?"

"This is the last place that I should suppose the famous Cologne water would come from," remarked Walter.

"Cologne water! O, that is just what I wanted," cried Minnie.

"Well, child, you can have as much as you want of that," replied her father.

"Where can we get it?"

"We can obtain it of Jean Marie Farina, the ——"

"That name I have seen on Cologne bottles; who was he?"

"He is the heir and successor of the original inventor of Eau de Cologne, or Cologne Water."

So, at the suggestion of Minnie, they all went to the store, and Mr. Percy bought a box of Cologne, consisting of six bottles, for which he paid one dollar and fifty cents.

The party remained two or three days in Cologne, and had a very fine time. They met there several Americans, and became acquainted with some of the residents. The children went into the cathedral every day, and it seemed as if Walter never would tire of the beautiful windows presented by the King of Bavaria. On the evening before leaving Cologne, as they sat looking out of their windows upon the Rhine.

covered with boats, and lighted with many colored lanterns, Mr. Percy said,—

"Our European tour is now nearly ended, and it becomes a question what we shall do. The time we intended to be absent has expired. We have spent in Europe as much time as we supposed would carry us through Europe and Palestine; and now the question is, whether we can give another winter to travel, and visit Eastern lands or not."

"I am for home," said Mr. Tenant; "we have given attention to the countries through which we have travelled, and I feel that my warehouse will not allow me to spend another winter away from it, however pleasant the tour would be."

"But shall we not see Palestine?" asked Walter. "I want to go home, and still I want to see the Oriental lands, about which we have heard so much."

"I would rather go home, and come out again," said Minnie.

"Well, friend Tenant," said Mr. Percy, "you have decided that you must go home."

"I think so."

"Well, children, I will tell you what I will propose."

"We shall readily fall in with your decision," said the lad.

"Of course," added his sister.

"Then I propose that we take a short route to London, and then to America; and if we live and prosper, I will give the children an Eastern tour in about two years. The two years will give them time for reading; they will be more mature in judgment and better able to make profitable the time we spend abroad."

"That is a good suggestion," remarked Mr. Tenant.

"And what say you, Walter?"

"That will suit me, only I don't want to give up the idea of going to Egypt and Palestine, at some time."

"Certainly not. But what does Minnie say?"

"O, it meets my wishes entirely. I want to see Cambridge, and mother, and little Charlie, who, I suppose, will be a large boy by this time."

"Then we will consider that decided, and I will make arrangements for an immediate return."

That night Mr. Percy sat down and wrote to a friend in London, asking him to secure passages for the party, in the steamer that was to sail on the 28th of August, from Liverpool to Boston. Having sealed his letter, he sent it to the post office, and it was soon on its way to London.

The next day at noon the party started in the cars for Antwerp. At Verviers, on the line between Prussia and Belgium, the passports were examined, and the baggage overhauled, the investigation being very light. In the evening they reached Antwerp, where they stopped that night. The next day they embarked on board the little steamer Rhine for London, at which place they arrived after a voyage of about sixteen hours. And glad they were to be once more in the metropolis of England, where the people seemed so much like those met at home.

On repairing to the hotel, Mr. Percy found a budget of letters, which he read with much interest. There were also letters for Walter and Minnie, and some for Mr. Tenant. During the day the following note from the gentleman to whom Mr. Percy wrote in relation to the passage home was received: —

Berkeley Square, Aug. 20, 1859.

Dear Sir: Your note came duly to hand, and the matter of business to which it related has been attended to. Your passage is engaged in the steamer Asia, Captain Lott, which sails on the 28th instant. Yourself and son will occupy one stateroom. Your friend will find a berth, No. 24, in a stateroom already occupied in part by an estimable English gentleman. Your daughter will share the stateroom of a Quakeress, who has kindly consented to attend to all Minnie's wants. I think you will all be comfortably situated, and trust you will have a pleasant voyage to your own America. Hoping that you will call on me before you leave, and as far as possible, make my house your home while in England,

   I subscribe myself, yours obediently.

"All right!" remarked Mr. Percy, on folding the letter.

"What?" asked Walter.

"Arrangements are made for our return; we go in the Asia, at the time set."

"Is the Asia a safe steamer?"

"Safe enough, but slow."

Having a few days left, the party travelled leisurely towards Liverpool, stopping on the way, and arrived at the great commercial city on the afternoon before the Asia was to sail. The evening was spent in making little purchases, and in carefully packing the baggage; and near midnight they all retired to rest, to dream of — HOME.

Chapter XVII.

HOMEWARD BOUND.

ONE beautiful Saturday morning, the whole party repaired to the steamship, which was anchored out in the Mersey, and were soon on board. All was hurry and confusion — passengers getting their baggage on board, tender farewell words being spoken, hurried messages delivered to those about to depart, and the merry songs of the seamen, who were attending to their duty on the deck.

At the time indicated, the moorings were cast off, and the steamer began to move down the River Mersey, which seemed alive with commerce, whitened by sails, cut into briny foam by tugs and drag boats, and restless beneath the uses to which it is put.

"Do you remember, Walter," said Mr. Percy, "the day when you sat on the pier yonder, and looked off upon the Mersey?"

"Yes, sir."

"Well, you have seen much and learned much since then."

"O, indeed I have."

"And now, as you are returning home, I want you to devise some way to deepen in your own mind the impression that has been made. This you can do by re-writing your journal, and adding such incidents as you may remember, by reading books which relate to the countries through which you have passed, and by writing out essays which you can hand to Mr. Falkner as your compositions in school. I will myself ask him to assign you subjects, in which you can avail yourself of the information you have gained."

"I will do as you tell me, father. I have already thought of several ways in which I can put my facts to valuable use."

"Do so, my son, and you will not have travelled in vain. Some people go through all the countries we have seen, and do not know any thing about them. They might as well have remained at home."

"I know it is so, for before I left home to come to Europe, I asked two or three men, who had been in Germany, Italy, France, and other countries, for information, and they did not know what to tell me. I then resolved that when I should be in distant lands, I would keep my eyes and ears open."

"Have you done so?"

"You will find out, in time. I have learned much more than you have any idea of."

The Asia was soon out at sea, and the dark night came on, many of the passengers were seasick, and among the rest Mr. Percy and Walter. Minnie and Mr. Tenant escaped without very serious illness. The voyage was of some interest, though not as pleasant as the one out. What occurred, and how Walter employed his time, the young reader may judge by the following passages from his journal: —

AT SEA, August 30, 1859.

We came on board on Saturday. I soon became sick, and took my berth, and have not had courage to crawl on deck until to-day — Monday. On Sabbath day no religious service was held on board, though father says there are several clergymen with us; but the passengers are nearly all seasick, and the steamer appears very dull, and many of the passengers have not yet left their staterooms. We are now pitching about, and I am hardly able to write, but felt a desire to fill out a few pages, hoping thereby I might turn my mind from the sickish feeling I have all the time.

As I wish to employ my time usefully on my way home, I have concluded to spend an hour each day in filling out some tables which will be of use to me hereafter, and I will employ my hour to-day in making out a table of the moneys of the countries through which we have passed, turned into federal money: —

		$	cts.	m.
ENGLISH.	Guinea,	5	00	0
	Sovereign,	4	84	0
	Crown,	1	10	0
	Shilling,	0	22	2
	Penny,	0	2	0
FRENCH.	Louis-d'or,	4	51	6
	Napoleon,	3	84	1
	Five Franc Piece,	0	93	0
	Franc,	0	18	6
	Sou,	0	1	0
AUSTRIAN.	Ducat,	2	27	0
	Sovereign,	4	84	0
	Rix Dollar,	0	97	0
	Florin,	0	49	0
PRUSSIAN.	Thaler,	0	69	0
	Rix Dollar,	0	69	0
HAMBURG.	Double Mark,	0	30	0
	Marc Banco,	0	35	0
	Rix Dollar,	1	05	0
TUSCAN.	Crown,	1	06	0
NEAPOLITAN.	Ducat,	0	80	0
LOMBARDIC.	Lira,	0	10	0

This table I shall make more perfect some other time. But, O dear me, I feel so seasick. I must lay down my pen.

Aug. 30, 1859.

Pleasant day on the ocean; not a sail in sight; no incidents; and for the want of something to do, I have been seeking out the pronunciation of some of the names of cities and towns which I find in my journal, (and which the reader will find in this series of books,) and here is the best I have been able to do:—

Maynooth,	*pronounced*	ma-nôth'.
Drogheda,	"	drŏh'e-da.
Armagh,	"	ar-mä'.
Garroch,	"	gar-ŏk'.
Loch Lomond,	"	lŏk-lō'mond.
Loch Leven,	"	lŏk-lĕv'en.
Lahore,	"	la-hōr'.
Trafalgar,	"	träf-al-gär'.
Thames,	"	tĕmz.
Woolwich,	"	wûl'ij.
Warwick,	"	wŏr'ik.
Calais,	"	kä-lā'.
Paris,	"	pär-ē'.
St. Cloud,	"	säng-klŏ'.
Versailles,	"	ver-sälz'.
Brussels,	"	brŭs'elz.
Scheldt,	"	skĕlt.
Cologne,	"	ko-lōn'.
Haarlem,	"	här'lem.
Enkhuizen,	"	enk-höï'zen.
Hague,	"	hāg.
Kiel,	"	kēl.
Prague,	"	präg.
Vienna,	"	vi-ĕn'a.
Trieste,	"	tri-ĕst'.
Ticino,	"	ti-chē'nō.
Bereguardo,	"	bä-rä-gwär'dō.
Buffalora,	"	bôf-a-lō'ra.
Novara,	"	no-vä'rä.
Romagnano,	"	ro-män-yä'nō.
Sesia,	"	sä'se-ä.

Lago Maggiore,	pronounced	lä′gō ma-jō′rä.
San Giorgio,	"	săng-jör′jō.
Pontecurone,	"	pŏn-tā-cô-rō′nä.
Valenza,	"	vä-lĕn′zä.
Mont Cenis,	"	mŏng-sā′ne.
Susa,	"	sŏ′sä.
Torino,	"	to-rē′nō.
Geneva,	"	ge-nĕ′va.
Oberstein,	"	ō′ber-stīn.
Oberwald,	"	ō′ber-vält.

O dear, I am tired of this, and must put away my writing for to-day. The steamer is pitching terribly, and I begin to feel seasick.

Sept. 3, 1859.

The weather is quiet to-day, and the steamer is ploughing through the waters at a rapid rate. But we are having a long passage. I this morning had a talk with Captain Lott, who gave me much valuable information about ocean navigation. He seemed pleased that I should ask him so many questions, and told me he had not seen a lad for years who seemed so willing to learn. I told him that that was what father took me abroad for — *to learn*. He replied, "If you ask as many questions of every body as you do of me, and remember all the answers that are given you, you will learn more than most men do, who visit Europe." He then asked me where we had travelled, what places we had seen, and I thought was trying to quiz me a little, to see how much I knew about the places we have visited. I am amused to see how many people treat boys as if they did not know any thing. Some men, who tell me stories, talk to me as if I could understand words of one syllable only. And many of the books written for boys, are written as if we did not know how to think. Hum! — to use one of Minnie's words.

Sept. 8, 1859.

Here we are, sailing into Halifax; the whole place is hung with banners, and is lively with music and merriment. I am told that the occasion of all this is a regatta, which is to take place in the spacious harbor. The boats, beautifully decorated and finely manned, are all ready, and soon they will set off. The steamer usually stops about two hours in this place to take in coal, but to-day we shall be obliged to stop six hours to get in coal and to take out the baggage and freight, as men are so much engaged in the regatta that they cannot be hired to work. Four or five of the employees of the steamboat company are all who will do any thing. Well, it is an ill wind that brings no good. We shall have an opportunity to see the regatta, and find out something about the people of Halifax. I must drop my pen — father is calling me to go up into the town a while. The day is a very fine one, and we shall enjoy it much. So here I go.

Sept. 9, 1859.

We shall arrive in Boston to-night, and O, how happy we shall be! On the day we started from Liverpool I made an estimate of the distance we should sail each day. I find that the calculation was wrong. It might have done for the Persia, but not for the Asia. I will give the estimate and the real progress. We sailed at noon on Saturday.

			Estimate.	*Real Sailing.*
To Sunday noon, August	29,	250	223
" Monday " "	30,	255	220
" Tuesday " "	31,	265	200
" Wednesday " September	1,	275	200
" Thursday " "	2,	280	202
" Friday " "	3,	285	230
" Saturday " "	4,	285	226
" Sunday " "	5,	295	254
" Monday " "	6,	300	264
" Tuesday " "	7,	300	278
" Wednesday " "	8,		220
" Thursday midnight "	9,		360
			2877

So I have made a great mistake in my reckonings, and have been two or three days on the water longer than I expected; but we shall be at home to-night.

About nine o'clock at night the Asia passed the lower light, and went on towards the city, The children were both on deck, and anxious to get ashore; and soon they saw in the dark night the outlines of the city, with its chimneys and steeples looming up before them. It was so dark that the steamer was a long time getting up to the pier, but those on board could see a crowd of friends on the shore, but could not distinguish them. At length the stern of the steamer came near the wharf, and a gentleman, getting upon the railing of the pier, shouted,—

"Is Mr. Percy on board?"

"Yes, sir," replied the gentleman named.

"Are all well?"

"Yes."

"Who is it?" asked Walter.

"Uncle Winthrop."

"Ah, uncle Winthrop! How do you do? How is mother?"

"Well."

"And Charlie?"

"Well."

"Is mother there?"

"No."

"Walter!" shouted a new and more juvenile voice.

"What?"

"I say, Walter!"

"Who is it?"

"Don't you know my voice?"

"No."

"Can't you tell who it is?"

"No. Who is it?"

"Harry St. Clair."

"Ah, Harry, how do you do?"

"First rate."

"How is it that you are up so late to-night?"

"Father let me take Sorrel and come over after you. Your uncle Winthrop will take Mr. Tenant and your father, and I am to take you and Minnie. How is she?"

"Well, she is here, trying to climb up, where she can see something."

"Harry!" cried the girl.

"Hurrah, Min!"

"We will get on shore in a minute."

"I know it."

The steamer had now drawn up to the wharf, and soon the children sprang ashore, and in a few minutes the two gentlemen were seated in a carriage with uncle Winthrop, and the children were in the chaise with Harry St. Clair, who, notwithstanding some bad habits, was really a noble boy. On they went, across the ferry, up Hanover Street, on towards Cambridge. The way seemed long to the children, so eager were they to get home.

"Do you suppose mother will be up?" asked Minnie.

"Certainly," replied Walter.

"But you know it is late — after midnight."

"Mother knows that we are coming, and of course she will be up, ready to receive us."

Soon the house was in sight, and these children were clasped in the fond maternal arms, and the family, separated so long, was again united!

THE PERCY FAMILY IN EUROPE.

BY REV. DANIEL C. EDDY, D. D.

In Five Volumes, Beautifully Illustrated.

EXTRACT FROM THE PREFACE.

THE author proposes to follow a travelling party through the principal countries of Europe, into Egypt, Palestine, and Greece. Though the successive volumes will be connected in name and style, and will be issued as a serial, a few months intervening between them, each one will be complete in itself.

NOTICES OF THE PRESS.
VISIT TO IRELAND.

A large amount of pleasing information in a small compass. — *Salem Observer.*

Clear and accurate. — *Christian Mirror.*

Having been over most of the ground, we can bear testimony to the fidelity of most of the descriptions here given. — *Zion's Advocate.*

Written in a pleasing, conversational style. — *Boston Traveller.*

Exceedingly attractive in its style. — *Lowell Citizen.*

Written in an engaging style, and makes the scenery, geography, and manners and customs of Ireland, almost as vivid and familiar as if one was looking upon them with his own eyes. — *N. Y. Independent.*

Well worthy of a place in every juvenile library. — *Mich. Ch. Herald.*

The author shows a happy faculty of telling a story, which is at once amusing and instructive; and while it is free from childish nonsense, is at the same time adapted to young minds. — *Prov. Journal.*

A valuable and entertaining book. — *Keene Sentinel.*

Highly interesting to children. — *Christian Secretary.*

We hope the readers will be reckoned by thousands. — *Bee.*

Just the thing for young people. — *Franklin Dem.*

The author writes in a popular and graphic style, and brings out things which those who follow him in his travels will wish to know. — *Boston Recorder.*

The plan of the series is pleasing and attractive. A merchant with two children travels through the principal countries of Europe, seeing every thing worthy of note. We think this will be one of the most popular series of books for youth ever published. — *Boston Trans.*

NOTICES OF THE PRESS.

SCOTLAND AND ENGLAND.

One advantage possessed by Dr. Eddy is, that he has successively travelled over the ground which he pictures. The aim of the writer at a style above the merely childish, at the same time that it is simple and intelligible, is praiseworthy. The youth of our times are too well informed, and too well cultivated in the use of proper language, to require extreme simplifying. This has well been avoided; and the result is, a book that will be read with improving interest by young people generally. — *Watchman and Reflector.*

The letters received from home, the surprises, and the little incidents which come naturally along, give it quite the air of reality. — *Boston Advertiser.*

The author of these books is a descriminating observer, an easy, sprightly writer. Let parents be sure and find these rare books. — *Philadelphia Chronicle.*

This is the most interesting and instructive series of books for children we have met with for a long time. — *Christian Times.*

A very handsome volume of an entertaining and instructive series. — *N. Y. Observer.*

The plan of the series Mr. Eddy is carrying out extremely well, and while he writes so simply as to enlist the sympathies of his readers, he tells them much that is new. His style is attractive to youth, and the series will be successful. — *Sat. Evening Gazette.*

A work of merit and interest, inferior to none in the juvenile department. — *Herald of Liberty.*

Written in fine style, and in language perfectly intelligible to children. — *Fall River News.*

Very instructive and attractive. — *Ballou's Pictorial.*

The vividness of a good panorama. — *Lynn Reporter.*

Adapted to youth, yet will interest and instruct adult readers. — *Guide to Holiness.*

We hope our notice will induce some publisher to reprint it. — *London Freeman.*

In one very important respect, Mr. Eddy's books, it seems to us, are much superior to Abbott's; that is, they presume that a youth *knows* something, and that the young reader has a few grains of common sense, and can exercise his reasoning faculty. — *Milford Journal.*

The history and the descriptions of the different places are given in the simplest language possible, and much valuable information is imparted, drawn out, as it were, naturally by the pertinent questions of the little children. — *Illustrated News.*

Much reliable information, in a very small compass. — *Eastern Argus.*

Judging from the volume before us, the series will be as interesting as the Rollo Books. — *Christian Freeman.*

Simple and interesting style, well adapted to youthful minds. — *Bulletin.*

The excellent Percy series. — *Prov. Journal.*

NOTICES OF THE PRESS.

All the readers of the former book will be sure to possess this. — *N. Y. Chronicle.*

Here is a book for boys and girls, ay, and for old men, and if there are such things, old women too. Here at our own fireside with the "Percy Family," we can look at Scotland and England, and see something that is worth seeing between Glasgow and Dover; and here within sight of Bunker Hill, and within ear-shot of the Old South, we can peep into Windsor Castle, and pleasantly smile at the matrimonial squabbles of royalty.

Here we can read the size of St. Paul's, and read the inscription in the "Bloody Tower" of the Tower of London. Pleasant gossip here is with the Percy Family; and here are some pretty little wood cuts. Buy the Percy Family, papa, for Walter. Buy the Percy Family, mamma, for Minnie. — *Sat. Ev. Express.*

This is another instalment of Dr. Eddy's description of a tour in Europe, under the familiar style of dialogue between a father and his little son. The questions of the boy in regard to the wonderful sights that met his eye are so clearly and graphically answered by the father, as to bring the scenes before the mind of the reader with a vivid distinctness. The numerous illustrations add increased interest to the work. — *Christian Secretary, Hartford.*

Described in terms intelligible to the young. — *Ch. Observer.*

Free from childish nonsense, yet adapted to youthful minds. — *Salem Gazette.*

We predict a great success. — *Religious Herald.*

Much valuable information. — *Boston Post.*

Well calculated to interest young readers. — *Am. Bap.*

A very interesting and valuable series. — *Bangor Whig.*

It is well written. — *Hampshire Gazette.*

Those who have read it speak of it in the highest terms. — *Sentinel, Middletown, Conn.*

It is a book written for children, and contains many pleasant and useful accounts of scenes and manners abroad, as witnessed by a party of juveniles who are supposed to be companions on a journey. The plan of the book is a good one, and the author has so individualized his characters as to give their several comments each a special interest. — *Norfolk Co. Journal.*

The author is a distinguished clergyman, and in the present work his talents for graceful and captivating writing are well shown. It is a book for youth, for whose minds it is evidently fitted. — *City Items, Phila.*

The work is intended for juveniles, and details a tour through Scotland and England. It is written in a pleasing and instructive style, and is an excellent book to place in the hands of the young, who will gain an amount of information here which it would take months to acquire elsewhere. — *Am. Union.*

These books are well printed and illustrated, and should go into every family. They are valuable for young or old. — *N. Y. Post.*

NOTICES OF THE PRESS.

PARIS TO AMSTERDAM.

Truly a valuable collection of little books for little folks. — *Newark Daily Adv.*

Written in a sprightly, conversational style; a pleasant companion for young or old. — *Mich. Ch. Herald.*

The young will not fail to be pleased. — *Ch. Observer, Phila.*

Dr. Eddy is doing the youth of this generation good service. — *Beverly Citizen.*

The author will receive the thanks of multitudes of children. — *Olive Branch.*

Every family in which there are young persons who may expect to visit Europe one of these days, should have this book read in its midst. There could be no pleasanter entertainment for a long winter's evening. It is a kind of imaginary tour of Europe made by a family, is written by one who is thoroughly acquainted with the scenes that he describes, and its perusal would prepare one to make the same tour in reality with pleasure and profit. The chief value of the book is, that it teaches one *how* to travel in Europe with advantage. It opens the way like a skilful pioneer, and especially to France, which, to the generality of Americans, is almost a sealed book. We all know more or less of England, our mother country. Besides being our ancestral birthplace, it has fuurnished and is still furnishing us with much of our daily reading, while of the interior life of France we know but very little. We know even more of Switzerland and Italy than of France. It is time, then, for a nearer and better acquaintance; and this little book, which has been written with a clear understanding of the necessities of the case, may serve as an excellent introduction. Every young person who reads it now would find it a mentor and a guide in future years. — *Phenix, Brattleboro'.*

Wise discretion and discrimination have been used. — *Lowell Courier.*

It is sufficient recommendation to say that it is from the pen of Rev. D. C. Eddy, of Boston. — *Worcester Daily Times.*

Great variety of information in a pleasing style. — *Atlas and Bee.*

The first two numbers of this series have been very successful, and the present volume is quite up to the mark of its predecessors. Aided by very neat engravings, the text describes, in narrative form, the numerous interesting sights and curiosities of Paris and Amsterdam, conveying a clear idea of them to the juvenile reader. The style is spirited and lively, and many pleasant anecdotes are introduced. Books like these have a high educational value; they prepare young readers for more elaborate works, and produce impressions of localities and manners that are never obliterated. — *Welcome Guest.*

The reader is here taken through various places of interest in France, Holland, and Belgium. The chapters on "French Royalty" and the "Field of Waterloo" are worthy of special mention, as conveying in a nutshell a large amount of political and historical information to the ready comprehension of the youthful reader. The series thus far is meeting with deserved appreciation. — *Boston Congregationalist.*

NOTICES OF THE PRESS.

Admirably adapted to old and young. — *Am. Union.*

A manner calculated to interest and please, as well as instruct the young. — *Sat. Evening Gazette.*

Mr. Eddy has a vigorous style, which imparts interest to whatever he writes. Then he has the happy faculty, in his sketches, of seizing upon the commonalities of life, — just what the great mass of people want to know about, — and presenting them with the air of naturalness. This is manifest in the little volume before us, which will be read with interest. — *Christian Era.*

Very attractive to the young. — *Home Monthly.*

It needs no commendation to those who have read the previous numbers. — *Mother's Journal.*

The Percy Family will prove prime favorites with the young, for they are on an extensive tour in Europe, and the account of their experience is entertaining and instructive. The first two volumes of the series have met with great success, and the third takes the travellers through a very interesting region. The illustrations also are novel and excellent. The narrative is lively, and makes the reader almost feel that he is one of the party. The series will give the little stay-at-homes a vivid impression of a trip to and through Europe. — *Salem Register.*

Well fitted to the taste of the young, and adapted to do them good by interesting them in real scenes and incidents. — *Boston Recorder.*

Very entertaining volumes. — *Western Watchman.*

Interesting and edifying. — *Prov. Post.*

The plan of *The Percy Family* series is excellent, and should be very popular. — *Leslie's Illustrated.*

We are weary of the monotony of successive books of travel, telling us only that "one more unfortunate" has used his eyes in favorable localities to very little purpose, and returning, wielded his pen with even less. A Boston book firm are publishing a series of travelling sketches on a different plan. The writer, Rev. D. C. Eddy, the well-known Baptist preacher, takes his representative tourists, the Percy family, over the familiar ground, and narrates their impressions of whatever, in each locality, is fitted to invite the attention of an intelligent man, or to touch the heart of a kind one. The young Americans of the party, with an inquisitiveness proper to the sex of one and the age and nation of both, draw from their elders just the facts and illustrations we are glad to meet, and which leave clearer ideas of scenes worth remembering than many a more ambitious production. — *Springfield Republican.*

It strikes us as an admirable plan, admirably executed, for carrying young people on foreign travels without leaving their own firesides. The father and his children are making the tour from Paris to Amsterdam. About all the novelties the children ask questions, and the father explains; and much information is given in the most attractive way. We commend the pretty book to our young readers. — *Presbyterian.*

This book is written in a style peculiarly pleasing, and the author has done a good service for the rising generation. We are glad to see the childish nonsense which often fills such works left out, and solid, useful information substituted. — *Troy Whig.*

THE BALTIC TO VESUVIUS.

A rare volume of the "Percy Family" series, entitled "The Baltic to Vesuvius." It is an interesting account of a journey from Prussia to Italy, well adapted to attract the minds of the young. — *Boston Transcript.*

The fourth volume in this interesting series has been published, and carries the reader through a portion of Europe full of scenes of interest, local, personal, and historic. These the author has sketched in a familiar and brief manner, which at once engages the attention. The popularity enjoyed by the first two volumes of this work, published, we think, about a twelvemonth since, must secure for the present issue an extensive circulation. The neat and attractive volumes now before us, however, have their own intrinsic and peculiar merits. After a careful perusal of their contents, we have no hesitation in pronouncing them superior to their predecessors. The historical references are read with greater interest, from their intimate connection with current events; and the incidents of travel, and anecdotes of personal adventure in and about Rome, Naples, Venice, &c., relating to such prominent characters as Victor Emmanuel, Garibaldi, &c., give the narrations life and freshness. — *Watchman and Reflector.*

The children are indebted to the author for another handsome, sketchy, readable book. We have never met with any series of books for the young into which so much general and historical information for children is crowded. There is amusement enough to carry the reader along without flagging, and yet the obvious design of the writer is to store the minds of his youthful friends with something of solid benefit. — *Express.*

This is the fourth of Mr. Eddy's series of books on foreign travels, written expressly for children. The plan is a happy one, and has been thus far most successfully carried out. The travelling party consists of Mr. Percy, his son and daughter, and another gentleman. In this volume are recorded sketches of their visits to several of the principal cities in the Old World; among them Hanover, Hamburg, Venice, Naples, Rome, &c. It is embellished with eight beautiful full-page engravings. — *Christian Visitor.*

Has woven his travels in Europe into a very interesting little volume for juveniles. The Percy Family, which figures in the tour, consists of a very affectionate and sensible father, and two wonderful children, a son and daughter. Between the questions of the children and the stories of the father, and others who happen to be in the company, the geography and history of the most interesting cities and places in parts of Europe are communicated in a way to interest children deeply, and give them many important lessons, which they would not get from historical works or books of travel. The idea of issuing such a book is a good one. The stories are well told, and the book will be popular. It will make an interesting holiday present. The tone of it is healthful, and the information it contains valuable. — *American Baptist.*

A pleasant book for young readers. — *Providence Daily Journal.*

NOTICES OF THE PRESS.

The author has a style peculiarly adapted to interest the young; he tells the prominent points in the history of every place his characters visit, in a simple, straightforward manner, which is calculated to improve the memory while it amuses his young readers. The *Percy Family* is really a most amusing and instructive series, and we can commend it warmly to our young friends. — *Illustrated Newspaper.*

Another of these sensible and attractive volumes for the young. It is a very interesting book for all classes of readers. — *Palladium, New Haven.*

This series of books, narrating the adventures of a family travelling in Europe, have been very acceptable to young readers. The history and geography of the places through which the travellers pass are given in familiar dialogues between the children and their parents. — *Boston Daily Advertiser.*

The fourth volume of an interesting and attractive series of juveniles. With no approach to dry and irksome detail, the author exhibits a happy faculty of imparting valuable geographical and historical information of the various localities. — *Congregationalist.*

This is a beautiful volume, and is one of a series of books designed for children. It is written in a graceful, pleasing style, and is just what will satisfy the young folks. — *Wide World.*

www.ingramcontent.com/pod-product-compliance
Lightning Source LLC
Chambersburg PA
CBHW021408230426
43666CB00006B/675